What people are saying about ...

NEVER SAY NO

"In my life, my parents have been equally counselors, companions, navigators, coconspirators, and friends. They've been a source of wisdom not only for me but also for our entire extended community. I'm excited that the simple parenting truths they've learned can reach even further through this book."

Tim Foreman, Switchfoot

"When I was young, I remember thinking that I had great parents but didn't really know what that meant. The memories return like a blurry ride. On the day my daughter was born, my wife and I began a different blurry journey—one where the stakes are high, sleep runs low, and time is of the essence. This book has given me a road map to see the past from my parents' perspective. And for new parents like myself, it offers landmarks of guidance to help map out the foreign terrain of parenting."

Jon Foreman, Switchfoot

"One of the scariest things that can happen to us is having kids. *Never Say No* brings hope to parents who are looking for a way to move forward. Instead of trying to control and shape kids' behavior, Mark and Jan have embraced another way, asking themselves: *Who will these children become and how can I help that happen in a beautiful way, while protecting them in the process?* Like seeds in the ground that we're watering, we're discovering with them and God who these kids actually are. This philosophy gives parents a strong offense that is a great balance to many other voices that we hear. Behavior is going to follow relationship. This counterintuitive approach to parenting can make a huge difference."

Donald Miller, author of *Blue Like Jazz*
and founder of The Mentoring Project

"*Never Say No* is a wise, holistic, and wonderfully inspiring book about the great work of opening up the world to children and cheering them on to the life God has for them as adults. Mark and Jan are not perfect parents announcing their success stories and 'how we did it right.' Far from it. They do, however, perfectly illuminate and embody the faithful, imaginative life of raising creative, empathetic citizens ready to contribute 'good' to the world. And for this, they'll forever have our gratitude and respect. For almost twenty years our lives have been entwined with the Foremans, in particular with their sons, Jon and Tim of the band Switchfoot. This represents a treasured place in our own individual stories. The Foremans' family story perennially reminds us of God's grace and the good fruit of intentional, Christ-dependent parenting."

Andi Ashworth, author of *Real Love for Real Life* and
editor in chief of the *Art House America* blog and
Charlie Peacock, Grammy Award-winning record
producer (Switchfoot, The Civil Wars, Chris Cornell)

"Rebekah and I go to one source for parenting advice: Mark and Jan Foreman. Their stories of raising sons who use their gifts to pierce the darkness will make you laugh and cry, and will also give you a glimpse into how to connect to your child's heart."

Gabe Lyons, author of *The Next Christians*
and **Rebekah Lyons,** author of *Freefall
to Fly*, cofounders of Q Ideas

"As new parents, my husband and I are always on the lookout for solid parenting wisdom. So needless to say, I was excited when I learned that my friends Mark and Jan had written a book about their inspiring journey as a family! Filled with practical insights, humor, and fantastic stories, *Never Say No* is a book I loved reading and one that I thoroughly recommend!"

Rebecca St. James, singer and
author of *One Last Thing*

"*Never Say No* taps into a powerful but neglected place—the landscape of imagination. Imagination connects us to eternity, allowing us to think, dream, and become. This book is a catalytic resource for parents and for everyone else."

John Sowers, president and CEO of The
Mentoring Project and author of *The Heroic Path*

"I've had the privilege of knowing Jon and Tim Foreman for the last fifteen years. While no simple formula could give birth to Switchfoot, when you meet Mark and Jan, the whole thing does start to make sense. Mark and Jan lead and love with kindness, humility, wisdom, and grace. I hope to be a dad someday—a dad like Mark. And when that day comes, I'll certainly be reaching for this book."

Jamie Tworkowski, author of *If You Feel Too Much* and founder of To Write Love on Her Arms

"The wisdom Mark and Jan share with us in these pages is pure gold. I can't wait to share this with every parent I know. Their message is more authentic because I still see them interacting with Jon and Tim in this way. A few years back, I walked out of a local coffee shop and ran into Mark and Jon outside. They were standing close and were clearly in a deep and trusting discussion. Their body language painted a beautiful picture of the closeness a parent and child can have. As a man who hopes parenthood is in his future, this book makes me more excited to enjoy the process of growing with my kids."

Patrick Dodd, singer and songwriter

"I'm so excited about this game-changing book and the impact it will have on leaders, parents, families, churches, and communities. Mark and Jan Foreman have not only raised two great sons but have also 'parented' many others over the years. Looking at the art and science of parenting in a whole new way, their wisdom, lessons, and practical perspective are timeless and much needed. Developing leaders first starts with developing your kids at home. Read this book!"

Brad Lomenick, author of *The Catalyst Leader* and former president of Catalyst

NEVER

SAY

NO

MARK & JAN FOREMAN

PARENTS of JON AND TIM FOREMAN of SWITCHFOOT

NEVER

SAY

NO

raising big-picture kids

David C Cook®

transforming lives together

NEVER SAY NO
Published by David C Cook
4050 Lee Vance View
Colorado Springs, CO 80918 U.S.A.

David C Cook Distribution Canada
55 Woodslee Avenue, Paris, Ontario, Canada N3L 3E5

David C Cook U.K., Kingsway Communications
Eastbourne, East Sussex BN23 6NT, England

The graphic circle C logo is a registered trademark of David C Cook.

The website addresses recommended throughout this book are offered as a
resource to you. These websites are not intended in any way to be or imply an
endorsement on the part of David C Cook, nor do we vouch for their content.

Unless otherwise noted, all Scripture quotations are taken from the Holy Bible,
New International Version®, NIV®. Copyright © 1973, 2011 by Biblica, Inc.™
Used by permission of Zondervan. All rights reserved worldwide. www.zondervan.
com; NASB are taken from the New American Standard Bible®, Copyright ©
1960, 1995 by The Lockman Foundation. Used by permission. (www.Lockman.
org); and NLT are taken from the Holy Bible, New Living Translation, copyright
© 1996, 2007 by Tyndale House Foundation. Used by permission of Tyndale
House Publishers, Inc., Carol Stream, Illinois 60188. All rights reserved.
The author has added italics to Scripture quotations for emphasis.

LCCN 2014948806
ISBN 978-0-7814-1173-8
eISBN 978-1-4347-0897-7

© 2015 Mark and Jan Foreman
The authors are represented by Sandra Bishop of MacGregor Literary, Inc.

The Team: Alex Field, Nicci Jordan Hubert, Amy Konyndyk, Nick
Lee, Jack Campbell, Helen Macdonald, Karen Athen
Cover Design: FaceOut Studios, Emily Weigel
Cover Photo: Getty Images, Robin Skjoldborg

Printed in the United States of America
First Edition 2015

1 2 3 4 5 6 7 8 9 10

030315

This book is dedicated to our two wonderful sons, Jon and Tim, whom we were privileged to parent and are now honored to call friends, along with their wives. We also dedicate this book to the next generation, our delightful grandkids whom we are crazy about, as well as to the previous generation—our inspiring moms and dads. We are especially grateful to the community, the friends and family who were and are part of our story. Finally, we dedicate this book to the gracious God who patiently taught us about Himself that we might imitate His love.

CONTENTS

INTRODUCTION

"Give us one nugget of parenting advice before you go," asked one of a half-dozen young leaders meeting with Mark at a local café.

"Okay," he said, "try out this one: never say no."

The room erupted with laughter, as the young dad looking for help reacted, "You *are* kidding, right? That's all I ever say—and my son needs one thousand more noes."

"No, I'm not kidding," Mark quietly responded. The room's mood sobered as each parent leaned forward to listen. "Never say no to all the dreams and creative ideas your children have. Never say no to the realization you can become different than your mom or dad. Especially never say no to your kids' requests to join them, like playing dress up with your little girl or going surfing with your teenager when the weather's cold and windy. If you say no too often, they'll stop asking."

A week later that concerned dad tracked Mark down to say he had taken that advice and his home life had dramatically turned around. "My son is suddenly easy to get along with just because I started saying yes to some things he wanted to do together. I'm not kidding," he said with a big grin. "The change is dramatic." As he walked away, he turned and pointed to Mark, saying, "It's hard, but never say no!"

No is a commanding word. It can be a denial, a rejection, an expression of fear, or an unintended statement of worth. But a thousand noes can be dwarfed by the power of one yes. We say yes to the stuff and people we value.

Most of us said "Yes!" when we discovered we were having children. The yes continues every time that baby needs feeding or changing or to be held. But that initial yes can be quickly dampened in a no world with all the challenges of raising small people.

But really, *never* say no? The title of this book is a hyperbole to startle our souls. We want to change the focus, to look at parenting through a different lens. Instead of targeting behavior, we want to step back and see what matters most: the relationship.

This shifts our perspective from a negative scrutiny of children's conduct to positively enjoying our kids. We believe strengthening an authentic bond between parent and child leads to cooperation in all areas of life. So we aren't endorsing permissiveness or leniency—far from it. We just hope to move beyond reactionary noes to proactive yeses. Behavior often takes care of itself when we focus on having a healthy relationship.

Of course, never say no is a dangerous phrase for the smothering or over-responsible parent. So increasing anyone's nervous control or guilt is not intended. We also don't endorse making a child the bright sun of the family universe, indulging every immature wish. No child can truly know who he or she is by looking within, living solely for self. Our narcissistic culture is shrinking our kids because when everyone is special, no one really is. We all need an outside reference point: to love and be loved.

Our children need to see their meaningful roles in a bigger story that is outside of their small lives. It's the grand scheme of a loving

God who says yes to having eternal relationships with us. Each family is a procreator of this incredible purpose. When kids realize they are part of God's enormous caring design, they find their true identities. As they lose themselves in loving God and others, they learn who they really are. This opens up more possibilities than anyone could imagine as they discover the yes of God for their own lives. This is what it means to raise big-picture kids.

Our story begins with how we discovered this paradigm shift from being right to celebrating relationship. It is our journey into learning to say yes to the loving plans of God for our kids and us.

How did we never say no in our family? What could yes look like in raising kids? We approach parenting from three directions:

- It begins with us
- A place to grow
- Launching into life

The starting point is with us, the parents. Then we describe never saying no in our home environment and community. Finally, we discover the giant yes of launching our children into the outer space of adult life.

One pressured dad complained to us that he did *not* want to begin a parenting conversation by looking at himself. He wanted easy, practical tricks to calm his wild children, not to confront his own blind spots. It's always more fun to pick out paint colors for a room than check its footings. This book allows readers to jump to any chapter or section, to scratch where they are currently itching. But since foundations support the whole house, we begin with us.

What is our purpose in parenting anyway? This is our initial paradigm shift as we turn from pursuing the very basic goals of a child's safety, success, or happiness to nurturing a big-picture child who loves well.

The shift continues as we honestly look at the noes in our lives, revisiting our families of origin and how we've inherited more than furniture or freckles from our parents and relatives. Having kids gives *us* fresh permission to grow up. And as we absorb God's love and delight for us, we are able to authentically translate that love to our children, to enjoy them for who *they* uniquely are.

The yes becomes more detailed in part 2 as we walk through the structures and rooms of our kids' world. How can we nurture our children's creativity, spirituality, and character through our homes, relationships, and words? One surprising bonus: Kids not only push us toward finally growing up but also pull us back into rediscovering childhood, to view life through their inquisitive eyes. Growing up doesn't have to mean growing old at heart. Children breathe the fresh air of wonder, and we can use this eager curiosity to shape their souls for what happens next.

Perhaps the most challenging yes is the final phase, when we release our older children to leave our carefully built home. Learning to say yes earlier can smooth this transition and create the most fulfilling season of all as we watch the metamorphosis of child to adult.

This stage may also find parents pushing the brake pedal through the floor as they ride helplessly in the backseat. We will talk about how to say yes to an adolescent's dreams, to cheer from the sidelines, and especially how to continue a close adult-to-adult relationship for the rest of our lives. Above all, we want to be remembered as never saying no.

Saying yes is not our original idea. We stole it from God's playbook, in which He always finds ways to be with us. Jesus described a parent's worst nightmare about a young man who ran away from home and wasted his kind father's attention, time, and money. Still, the waiting father never said no to this lost child, and when his broken son finally dragged himself home, the dad screamed, "Yes!" and sprinted to embrace him—then he threw a party! We can adopt this story as our template for parenting.

Why did we write our story after thirty-seven years? This book is our attempt to answer the question we are most often asked: "How did you raise your kids?" It's actually a book we wish someone had written for us as insecure parents. We never saw ourselves as parenting authorities; we just knew we'd been given two phenomenal kids to be raised. It was more about not messing up God's ingenious creations.

We longed to shadow experienced moms and dads around their homes, to participate in a family reality show. This was in fact what Jan attempted to do after learning she was expecting our first son. She brashly invited herself to her boss's home to observe his wife with their newborn—and take notes. "Why am I ashamed to admit that I've never fed, bathed, burped, diapered, or even held a baby *ever* in my whole life?" Jan said. No one is born with this experience. She needed a demonstration.

The boss's wife, Betsy, graciously granted Jan's request and calmly handed over her two-month-old daughter, like one would pass a bag of groceries.

Predictably, in less than five minutes, the infant thrust her bottle out of her unhappy mouth and replaced her vigorous sucking with unearthly screams. Jan felt this little one was speaking for both of them.

Jan was filled with global doubts: *Am I not good with children? Did I completely fail my crazy experiment? More importantly, will I succeed as a parent?* Most of all, she realized she just needed more practice.

This book is an invitation to practice on our family: to enter our home, join our noisy mealtimes, walk down the hall, and listen to bedtime stories. Looking over our shoulders, you might be spared some of our mistakes or be encouraged to move in some new direction. Yes, we practiced on our own children and certainly discovered that practice does not make perfect parents or kids. But this is our imperfect story of how we raised two beloved sons.

Imagine waking up to discover a satellite has made a soft landing in your backyard. What is it exactly? How does it work? Where did it originate? What information does it hold? You begin to reverse engineer the strange arrival, taking it apart, piece by piece. You are looking for clues as a self-made engineer, to learn the intricacies of satellites. It's yours. It's in your backyard!

Reflecting on our adult sons, now married with kids of their own, and how they handle their public life with character, we feel like something wonderful landed in our lives. How did this happen? What shaped these men? This book is our attempt to reverse engineer the childhoods of Jon and Tim.

We use the term *engineering* loosely. This is not a blueprint for parenting; these are rough sketches of what we thought, did, and learned along the way. Nor is it an owner's manual with a promise of warranty if your model fails to operate properly.

As we reflect on our family odyssey, we find God's undeserved fingerprints everywhere. We do not claim to be model humans or parents, and we never placed that burden on our children, even now as adults. We fully admit that 100 percent of the outcome is simply grace. But with that said, we hope parents can be encouraged from our story, told through memories both playful and sobering, with hopeful lessons attached.

Raising children is the most humbling and exhilarating privilege on earth. Here's to saying yes!

Part One

IT BEGINS WITH ME

Granola is a staple in our house. We eat it for breakfast by itself or in pancakes, and by handfuls throughout the day. Jan makes it fresh every week and keeps it in a large jar by our fridge. On top of this container is a round gray stone with one word, hand painted, surrounded by flowers in green, blue, red, and white. That word is "Grace."

We don't remember how this little rock came to live at our house, but for years it has rested atop the granola jar. It's a reminder, a little obstacle, before we can reach into the delicious oats and nuts to eat the day's sustenance: Everything is grace. Be thankful. Give grace away.

Grace is at the center of our family, just as granola is an essential part of our diet. Yes, of course, grace is remembering to give thanks before a meal, a surf session, or safe arrival home. But grace is also the free hug from your child when you've been less than pleasant. It's laughing when the third glass of orange juice tips over at breakfast. Grace is not stating the obvious when your spouse's adamant insistence on where he or she left the receipt is proved wrong. It's walking slower to the tempo of small feet and legs, taking time to see the wonder from young eyes. Grace is listening with interest to the same story from your elders because they enjoy reliving that moment, not because you are entertained.

Our attraction to grace comes from another familiar story. We believe the story of Jesus, that God became one of us and met us in our own neighborhoods. He spoke our language and ate our food. He validated His love by demonstrating astonishing, supernatural grace: healing eyes, broken bodies, and souls. To remove all distance between us, He paid with His life for all the wrongs we've done. None of this came with an invoice. He gave because of grace.

This is the best place we know to look for that unconditional love we crave so desperately. We want this grace to flavor our lives. Hopefully, it changes how we respond to the big and little people around us. In order to scoop up the savory nourishment of living together as a family, we must hold on to grace.

It is all about grace.

Chapter 1

HEY, CAN THAT KID SWIM?

The Goal of Parenting

BY MARK

That Labor Day in Lake Arrowhead was picture-perfect, high above the smoggy oven of the Los Angeles basin. We wanted to capture on film our growing family of four. I found an ideal location on a secluded cove, fringed by mature pines with a generous beach. Twenty-two-month-old Jon bounced happily in his inflated yellow boat on the shore, while three-week-old Tim was waking up on a blanket stretched over pristine sand. The dry breeze was alive with the noise of summer's end, ski boats and blue jays competing for volume.

Like paparazzi, we fired our Instamatic camera as Tim wriggled on his back. First, a head-to-toe shot with his twig-like arms reaching for the sky, then a close-up of his tiny, perfect hand clasping my little finger. With all eyes on Tim, we wrongly assumed Jon was safe.

"Hey, can that kid swim?" a woman screamed from across the cove.

I quickly glanced at the vacant beach where Jon had been only minutes ago. Then in panic, I looked out to see his empty yellow boat floating upside down twenty-five feet offshore. Jon was underwater. Apparently a boat wake had silently swept his little inflatable into the water and flipped him over.

Heart pounding, I exploded into the water. Jon was floating vertically with his head about eight inches below the surface. Somehow he was instinctively holding his breath, his blue eyes wide open, looking up in patient trust. I snatched him out of the water, soaking wet with the smell of the lake, and held him tight.

Surprisingly, there were no tears. No gasping for air. Not even a whimper of anxiety. Jon loved the water and was having fun, unaware of the danger that had just passed. Not wanting to stir up fear, I kept my voice light and playful, hiding the inner trembling. But Jon's words pierced my calm facade: "I couldn't find you."

I felt relieved yet sickened. What was I thinking? How could Jan and I have taken our eyes off a toddler for that long? Did we even know what we were doing as parents?

We were approaching parenthood as casually as that photo shoot, expecting a tranquil world where we could control every circumstance. We could shelter our children in a protected cove, cushioned in an inflatable and nested on a soft blanket. But we couldn't predict the unexpected boat wake that almost capsized our world.

That night we gratefully tucked a drowsy Jon-Jon into bed and settled baby Timmy in his bassinet. But, sleepless, I lay limp in silence, staring at the ceiling, watching the shadows of windblown pines dance across our walls. My mind kept visualizing the empty beach, the floating inner tube, and Jon's trusting eyes. Echoing in my memory was the woman's startling, gracious cry that saved Jon's life. What could two inexperienced parents learn from this merciful intervention, this life lesson we hoped never to repeat?

I wish I could say that by night's end we both had visions of the perfect parent and a scroll dropped from heaven revealing ten steps for a model family. No more blind mistakes. But we did have a mini-epiphany, the first of many awakenings.

Jan and I realized we had been gifted with two sons; now we were re-gifted to love them a little longer. Jon and Tim were here by design, saved for a bigger picture beyond cute photographs on a beach.

We realized almost tangibly that God's hand was on both their lives, so we felt an urgency to find His fingerprints. It was as if God stepped into our cabin, embraced our two children, and reminded us that He had great plans for them. This was not parenting mega-lomania, but a truth for every child that had become clearer to us. Children are priceless. There must be an equally invaluable purpose for each life.

We began asking ourselves, what is the point of parenting?

Parenting without a Purpose

> *Alice: Would you tell me, please, which way I ought to go?*
> *Cat: That depends on where you want to get to.*
> *Alice: I don't much care where—*
> *Cat: Then it doesn't matter which way you go.*
> —Lewis Carroll, *Alice's Adventures in Wonderland*

Jan and I were teenage products of the tumultuous '60s. Our *Leave It to Beaver* world was turned on its head with assassinations, psychedelic drugs, free sex, violent protests, and the Vietnam War. With the innocent '50s of our childhood lost, we wondered if this world was even safe to raise kids.

We were not infatuated with babies. The responsibility was daunting. But in my last year of grad school, Jan's secretary job provided medical coverage for pregnancy, which was rare in the '70s. So for the greatest adventure of our lives, we had no clear direction, no point on the horizon toward which we were headed. We just thought it would be cool to have kids.

When one plus one became three, we tried on several basic goals, but none of them seemed adequate. Our initial objective came the minute we walked newborn Jon in the door from the hospital. It was pure survival.

We became obsessed with security and bought safety latches, gates, and outlet covers. We purchased nontoxic wooden toys and researched ingredients in packaged foods. Of course, our immediate reaction after Jon's near drowning was to enroll him in swim class. We tried to anticipate every worst-case scenario. We wanted safety! It is most parents' essential, entry-level strategy: keep the child alive.

But is safety a final goal? Should we get stuck here with our focus on preventing catastrophe?

Jan's earliest flip phone greeted her with this innocuous message: "Be safe, be courteous." Obviously, we wanted our home to be a secure nest for our children, both physically and emotionally. How easily that slogan can become a high watermark for us parents. We want our kids to live in safe neighborhoods, attend safe schools with

safe friends, and marry safe spouses. We want our kids to be good—
not naughty, but nice. Yet what is the point of holding a feverish
child all afternoon or re-mopping crumbs around the high chair or
staying awake until you hear your teenager come home at night? Our
frightening lake experience woke us to the fact that solely aiming for
protection is not really safe—or realistic. What are kids safe *for*?

And living next door to the goal of safety was healthy. As post-
hippies, we subscribed to the whole-foods culture: we ground our
own wheat, canned homegrown tomatoes, and joined an organic
co-op. Our mountain community was dotted with folks escaping
the deadly toxins of LA.

Ironically, we were not immune to the common colds and
frequent viruses of other young families, even though we abstained
from white sugar. All this effort caused us to ask: Is there life after
raw goat milk? Is our absorption with physical nourishment actually
unhealthy? Even if we are actually healthier than most, what are we
healthy *for*?

Another immediate need was simply to keep our baby from crying
so much, which can easily turn into the endless pursuit of happiness.
Let's keep the child happy so *we* can be happy. Our World War II
Great Depression parents worked to give us everything they lacked so
we would be perpetually amused. As boomers, we were cradled under
that blanket of happiness as one of our "unalienable rights."

Now it was our kids' turn; they were going to be twice as happy.
We could double their toys, their activities, their education—and
our expense. Without thinking, we found ourselves chasing this elu-
sive goal of pleasing our children—and connecting that bliss to what
we could purchase.

But do more toys equal more joy? Perhaps racing for this moving finish line actually robs our children of authentic joy. Just imagine a miserable generation collectively chanting, "Make us happy!" God is not afraid of our unhappiness and often does His best work when we are uncomfortable. He certainly does not give us everything we want.

Perhaps the holiest grail of basic parenting goals is that multi-faceted jewel called success. Jan and I wanted our children to "do well," whatever that means. Our search began within the first year when a friend's wiry ten-month-old daughter walked around our living room while our son crawled slowly from toy to toy. But, we calculated, our son could already say six words, and she still babbled. Success!

Or maybe success looks a lot like our fading aspirations: the symbolic football in the crib. Every child is wired to be great at a few things, but not everything. And how are we measuring that greatness? We usually boil it down to a few ingredients: physical appearance, material possessions, athletic ability, intelligence, or popularity.

And depending on our circle of friends, or what commercial we just watched, we could add other criteria.

We could also equate success with a four-letter-word: *busy*. If our calendar was filled, we must be competent parents. But the quantity of activities did not equal a quality of life. In fact, the more we bowed to busy, the more inadequate we felt as parents.

/// **SUCCESS DEFINED BY ALL THE YAPPING DOGS OF CULTURE IS A TYRANT FOR BOTH PARENT AND CHILD.** /// It blinds us from discovering our children's unique gifts. And we are not fun to be around.

These basic goals of safety, health, happiness, even success, are often too shallow to be admitted by conscientious parents. But they still lie beneath the surface, like tectonic forces, and shape how we parent. In a recent Harvard survey, 80 percent of youth said adults in their lives were more concerned about their success or happiness than caring for others. Ironically, in the same survey, the adults insisted that growing caring kids was their top priority. Obviously, there is often a gap between what we believe *should* matter and how we actually live.[1]

What we may consciously aim toward in raising our kids are two loftier virtues: self-esteem and good character. At first glance, it would seem that all the other shallow goals depend on these two qualities.

For half a century, many authorities insisted that a child's self-esteem must be the focus because without self-confidence a child cannot thrive. However, a recent study following those venerated children into adulthood showed no significant benefits. In fact, "indiscriminate praise might just as easily promote narcissism" and all of its negative consequences. Self-esteem alone is not enough.[2]

For good reason, character has become another revered parenting goal.[3] Who can argue with the importance of developing a child's conscience?[4] We want our children to withstand life's pressures, living from the inside out. Without an ethical compass, no child-turned-adult will have healthy relationships or vocational success.[5] But is the child merely "good for goodness' sake"?[6]

Without doubting these crucial qualities, is there a higher purpose still that even these virtues can serve? Like moving closer through concentric circles toward a bull's-eye, we want to find the central purpose that is uniquely human in each of our children. These other virtues may be worthy points on the horizon, but what greater good lies beyond?

A Purpose Emerges

*The purpose of life is not to be happy. It is to be useful,
to be honorable, to be compassionate, to have it make
some difference that you have lived and lived well.*
—Ralph Waldo Emerson

You are the salt of the earth.... You are the light of the world.
—Jesus

Jon's alarming rescue began the great unraveling of our status quo. Our protective, inward, and even selfish goals of safety, health, happiness, or success seemed nearsighted. Even self-esteem and good character begged for a grander explanation. It was time to question our parental GPS, to step away from the trees and be amazed by the forest, quite literally in the mountains!

I was a fan of Emerson before I was a follower of Jesus. But when I read Jesus's words about being salt and light to others, I was struck by a similarity and one difference. Both taught us to live beyond the borders of self. Emerson emphasized "making some difference." But Jesus went further to say we could intentionally change our surroundings for good. That light and salt are not neutral. The world will be better because we are here.

Jesus's salt and light metaphor explains God's parenting purpose for His own kids: to reflect God's loving nature to others. We can take our place in His radical plan to restore creation. Does this mean we can adopt this same purpose for our own children, to help them find their unique roles in God's courageous love story?

Before marriage, Jan and I considered ourselves edgy. When I proposed, I added this romantic disclaimer: "I can't promise we won't live in a VW bus under a bridge." The fact that Jan said yes proved she had her own radical agenda. Our married mission statement was "To be used to the greatest extent for the greatest good, to burn out rather than rust out." Not exactly a cozy motto to hang over the family fireplace, but it did kick our meandering parenthood in a certain direction. We gradually realized that our kids could be edgy too.

Jesus warned against parochial religion that plays it safe. /// **SO WE DID NOT WANT OUR KIDS CLOISTERED IN A RELIGIOUS TOWER, TRYING TO BEHAVE UNTIL HEAVEN.** /// We believed our children could play an important part in God's redemptive plan to bring heaven to earth. We imagined them spiritually propelled into society, equipped with the realization that they could, in some way, transform it.

We believed that Jon and Tim's unique gifts could best be discovered in the immensity of God's purpose rather than improvising small, isolated stories all about themselves. This bigger story is not just about us, and it didn't originate with us. It is best described in the familiar words "God so loved the world that He gave ..." God loved us in that particular way. Authentic love not only feels deeply but also acts courageously and sacrificially. Love gives.

God not only loved, but He loved the *whole world*. We can imagine God hugging the beautiful places of our wondrous blue planet. But God, through Jesus, crashed through religious and cultural barriers to embrace the hurting who hide in the dark corners of our broken, worn, and often brutal world. How could we then raise our children to be religiously insulated? Our kids, all kids, were made to taste this daring love, then give it away.

We all get to grow up and look like God—at least have some resemblance. Jan and I had created children in our image: Jon had my forehead; Tim, my brown eyes; and both inherited Jan's chin. Yet we are all being shaped by a common spiritual genetic code, God's own likeness. God's most distinguishing feature is His outrageous love. He can't leave us alone. He wants to sculpt us into wholeness, to repair our distrust, and to give us His view of others.

We wanted to help our kids break out of a flat self-focus to discover the three-dimensional face of God, receiving His dynamic love and then giving it away. Because we cannot be content by living only for ourselves. Hand in hand, parent and child can explore the surprising, tender, restoring love of God, beyond the borders of self.

This raises the bar for parenting and also takes the pressure off. We are not creating our own little stream. We are jumping into an immensely generous river that is already flowing and spans generations and continents. We are necessary parts in a redemptive story bigger than ourselves, to be the face of God to the person next to us. It gives new meaning to the question "Hey, can that kid swim?"

Saving the World with Elevator Parts

I like to imagine that the world is one big machine. You know, machines never have any extra parts. They have the exact number and type of parts they need. So I figure if the entire world is a big machine, I have to be here for some reason. And that means you have to be here for some reason, too.

—Brian Selznick, *The Invention of Hugo Cabret*

Purpose starts early. Our kids naturally sense this greater plan. When Jon was five and Tim just turned four, we moved into a seventy-five-year-old house. The previous owner was an eccentric retired elevator repairman. Oddly, whenever he had a spare part, small or large, he would bury it behind the house. Shortly after moving in, our kids made this exciting discovery. The yard became an archaeological dig for buried treasure.

We had transferred to a church that was thirty thousand dollars in debt. We talked and prayed openly about the problem of paying the overdue bills. Two small people with big hearts were listening.

One morning, Jon and Tim announced they had a plan for raising the money.

"We're gonna sell the elevator parts."

What could we say? They were willing to relinquish their new-found treasures. They saw themselves as part of the solution. Jan and I just raised our eyebrows, gave each other a look that said, "Let's see how *this* goes," and I said aloud, "Great!"

They quite literally had a yard sale. They worked all morning digging and washing the rusty mud off each mysterious part. Most had been buried for decades. Then they made price tags for each item; some went for twenty-five cents, but others they felt were worth at least five dollars. After they arranged all the parts on our front driveway, they made a giant sign that read "Elevator Parts for Sale. Help the Church."

Then they sat down on two plastic chairs and waited. And waited.

As grace would have it, they didn't wait too long. A familiar car pulled up to the curb. Two new friends had come to see how our move was going. But they were so impressed by the sea of elevator parts, each carefully labeled, they began to shop. The word spread throughout the day from these original shoppers, and by late afternoon, every single part was sold.

At the end of the day, Jon and Tim looked at us triumphantly and said, "See, you guys. We knew we could raise the money!"

We don't recall how much was raised, but the real value was in their growth of character through the process as they imagined, dug, polished, and gave. It's not just about what our kids *do* but who they *are*, or will become. What qualities are being nurtured in the heart? Our kids have brilliant ideas and the resources to move adult-size mountains. They want to see themselves in a larger adventure. /// EVERY KID WANTS TO MATTER. ///

Hey, Can That Kid Swim!

Jon's simple words when rescued were profound: "I couldn't find you."

We had lost each other in that moment, and almost forever. Our child's ability to swim was connected to *us*. Staying close to our children was critical not only for their survival but also for finding their purpose in life. We believed that as we fed and watered our relationship, we would grow our children's confidence to find themselves in God's big story.

Jon and Tim eventually took swimming lessons. It was not just to be safe on the shore. Our sons learned to love water, and they swam for pure enjoyment. In fact, one of Tim's first nicknames was Timmy-Swimmy.

When we guide our children into God's greater purpose for their lives, we notice a similar enthusiasm. To quote Eric Liddell, "God made me fast. And when I run, I feel His pleasure."

Learning to swim eventually allowed our kids to explore the once-dangerous lake. They learned to jump off docks, water-ski, and ride wakeboards. I read recently online that they swam across a small Midwest lake just for fun at a music festival. Swimming has certainly carried them to new worlds. They have been submerged in almost every ocean on the planet.

Like our desire for our children to be comfortable in the water, we want our children to be comfortable in the skin God gave them. We want them to confidently explore their purpose in a vast world. This is how God's big plan can transport our children to face the unfamiliar with courage. We can cheer wildly for them to travel beyond even our own comfort zones as parents. Gasp!

Now we are the ones watching from shore, figuratively in a crowded venue or literally as they glide down moving water-mountains taller than us, sometimes surfing on boards they themselves have shaped. We are still captivated by the graceful beauty of what some call "walking on water."

Peter's original version was miraculous. But so was the first time we held our newborn sons, or watched them take first steps, or saw them wave good-bye to us on the first days of kindergarten, then learn to drive, graduate, marry, and have their own families—all of this is beyond comprehension. And so is this amazing journey we continue to follow.

We like to turn that woman's alarming question around, into a wonderfully amazed exclamation: "Hey, can that kid swim!"

Questions

How would you describe your purpose as a parent?

What big-picture purpose do you envision for your child?

Are there lesser goals that could obscure this focus, such as success, fame, achievement, or happiness? Why might these be important to you?

How might these goals interfere with a higher purpose for your child?

Chapter 2

OUR LONG, WINDING ROAD

The Family Map

BY JAN

*I hold that a strongly marked personality can
influence descendants for generations.*

—Beatrix Potter

When our first son finally made his dramatic entrance, arriving two
weeks late after thirty-six hours of labor, an unspoken question arose:
Now what?

I had only two blurry days to get acquainted with Jon inside
the hospital confinement. Once released, I timidly cradled our nine-
pound treasure out of that sterile environment to the parking lot
where anything might happen.

At twenty-four years old, I had a tiny human forty-eight hours
new placed on my lap for his inaugural ride home. Looking back,

even this initial act seems hazardous, as hospitals now demand a car seat inspection, complete with installation ceremony. But over thirty years ago, my nervous arms were considered a sufficient safety restraint.

Car seat aside, was our child really safe with *us*?

I stared in wondrous disbelief at the beautiful blond head, resting, asleep in complete trust. As our borrowed Toyota Corolla exited the lot, leaving behind the medical experts, I began to cry. These were tears of joy mixed with a holy fear.

We drove in that profound silence for several minutes until we reached the outskirts of San Bernardino. Beginning the steep incline up Waterman Canyon, Mark started to sing. I gradually found my voice too, and the melody and familiar words carried us like a cradle, reminding us we were not alone on this journey.

We drove up a two-lane mountain road that was called the Rim of the World Highway because it meandered to five thousand feet with hairpin turns and steep cliffs. This familiar road led to our cabin, but we were beginning a new parallel journey to dizzying heights on a parenting road that would prove to be just as circuitous.

Later that night, I wrote:

I should have taken my cues from Jon's serene disposition at that moment. Instead, as we began the drive up the mountains on that lovely Sunday afternoon, I found great tears welling up in my eyes as I held that soft, warm life, his expression so peaceful and trusting.... I trembled to feel that little one in my arms and became like him in God's arms, totally leaning on Him for wisdom because I felt so inadequate. Yet God entrusted Jonathan to us, so we must be candidates for God's provision.

Jon was a child of our firsts: the first baby held, fed, diapered, and bathed. He was as inexperienced as his parents, and my tears betrayed our lack of confidence. We would have to grow up together.

Only two weeks prior, we had moved into an 875-square-foot cabin. I continued writing:

We came home to our new house. My, wasn't everything new! We felt numb. Mark had lovingly cleaned the house and put his surgical cap and mask on the stuffed dog in the nursery, remaking the bed with clean, pink sheets. I felt welcomed. Jonathan began to let his hair down, too, for it seemed that immediately upon arrival, he began to cry. Now in the perfect (unreal) setting of the hospital he had never cried with me, and at once I wished for those capable nurses to be here. Not exactly stable myself, I began to cry with him, so afraid at any minute I would do him (or had already done him) harm. Mark and I were together laboring over changing him—and I wondered: Will it always take two of us?

I like to believe most parents are similar: awkwardly excited, frightened yet exploding with eagerness to embrace this new life. Gradually, unceremoniously, we begin to explore the wilderness of parenthood, settling into a cadence on some obvious, cleared pathway. At a minimum, we simply rework the trails of our own parents, who perhaps imitated their fathers and mothers. Our generational steps are unintentionally learned, so family traits are easily recycled.

Yes, everything about our newborn was *new*. But we were not new. At twenty-four years, we had inherited some mileage.

Tucked into the back pocket of our souls, out of sight but easily grabbed, were well-worn maps. We each carried our own inherent responses to all things family. We bought a new crib, stocked the nursery with the latest toys, and filled Jon's dresser with unworn outfits. Still, the tired, ingrained habits of previous generations crept uninvited through our windows. And we were shocked to hear our mothers' or fathers' words in our minds or through our voices. We were not the only adults residing in our home.

So within months, we were forced to scrutinize our relational DNA. We began to notice familial patterns, boundaries, roles and rules, tones and gestures, and involuntary reactions that were not original. We had to admit it: our relatives had taught us how to relate.

A helpful tool called a genogram can trace a family's tree back two or three generations. It graphically describes any character traits, relational dynamics, and reoccurring problems within our branches. It's illuminating for us to stand back and see our trees in the forest.[1]

But we never formally sat down to draw up a list of our individual family traits, which would have been insightful. Rather, we were tripping over the inherited relics throughout the day. Raising our children was regurgitating our past. /// **IN ORDER TO MOVE FORWARD, WE NEEDED TO GLANCE BACKWARD AT HOW WE WERE PARENTED.** ///

It's intriguing to look back two or even three generations. We often find ourselves trailing behind the long shadows of ancestors: my grandmother played ragtime piano for Wartrace, Tennessee, dances; another relative led worship on guitar; my father was a choir director; and Mark's grandmother played violin. Musical aspiration was never scripted in our family, but easily assumed. How did this happen? Organically through stories and shared experiences, we passed along what we enjoyed. This is how we adopt the patterns of our families, like a tree sprouting limbs from its roots.

And certainly there was much to preserve from the familial past. Mark is a third-generation Californian who appreciates his pioneer heritage of outspoken risk takers. I'm grateful for generations of believing relatives who faithfully served God and their communities—and for my Swedish family dessert recipes!

But we had to admit that some of our beaten paths were dark, sinister alleys that we hoped never to revisit. Driven by idealistic, youthful arrogance, we audaciously hoped to discover the mythic land of the Perfect Family, far from our original flawed homes. We believed we could improve on the established, rutted paths of previous generations. But charting a new course proved challenging. It's not easy to recognize and then commence roadwork on well-paved habits.

Redo, React, or Rewrite

Even in our first year of marriage, before kids, we found discrepancies in our personal maps. Most of these conflicts were innocuous: who takes out the trash or pays bills, finding friends we both enjoyed, or how often to visit parents. But after we had our first child, more serious differences surfaced. Our two road maps became roadblocks that revealed very different histories—and destinations. We began to wrestle with the good, bad, and ugly of how we were raised and the implications for our innocent child.

Combining our opposite backgrounds seemed impossible: Mark was raised in a Guns N' Roses family: blunt, loud conversations often led to shoot-outs but were followed by ample hugs and kisses.

My family style was more like the Chiffons: soft-spoken and pleasant but avoiding confrontation at the cost of authentic relationship.

Our parents were equally polarized: Mark's mom was fun-loving and outgoing but emotionally unpredictable. My mom was kind, practical, reserved, and disciplined.

Our fathers were also opposites: Mark's dad was a successful, bright engineer, physically present but often preoccupied, showing affection by teasing. My dad was creative, intelligent, fun, and engaging but could be a perfectionist at times.

Which model would work for our children? We were obviously not our parents so none of these combinations of traits appealed to us for our kids. Our growing discontent became a springboard to find new destinations and ways to arrive.

We faced two perils for our clashing histories—we could *redo* or we could *react. Redoing* meant that one of us would seemingly win, and the other, lose: Do we celebrate that holiday exactly following your traditions or mine? Will I ignore your preferences for social limits or just plan out the week myself? Your mom only supervised the kids, but mine worked full-time, so that is my choice.

We soon learned that when only one person dictated the rules of the road, we both lost.

On the other hand, *reacting* would completely dismiss any good we might have learned from our parents and could create imbalance in other areas: Our parents were distracted and rarely invested time in our interests, so let's make our kids the center. Our childhood lives were boring and predictable, so we will compensate with a glut of toys and activities. Our parents were too religious, so let's create our own spirituality at home.

/// **THE BETTER BUT MORE STRENUOUS COURSE WAS** *REWRITING* **A NEW MAP — TOGETHER.** /// This would combine our favorite memories while hopefully avoiding the dreaded pitfalls of our past. This new collaboration would enrich our family the most.

My ancestry was homogeneously grown inside the church. Mark's relatives were colorful agnostics or nominal believers, most of whom arrived dramatically on faith's doorstep during the '70s. We could draw from years of faithfulness *and* stories of miraculous redemption.

It's fascinating that genetics teaches the same lesson. Biologically, children are neither just like their mom nor their dad but are brand-new combinations of traits. In the same way, each family creates a new us that is unlike any other family. If we add the promise of a new creation in Christ, we can include the dimension of God's likeness coming into our homes. Now the possibilities are endless. We can look back on our past or to our future with bright expectations.

Our hopeful home began here: believing that God could re-create us and those we loved. If we merely coasted on our default settings, the future would be predictable: we would become our parents. Or simply reacting to our past would keep our new home still in its negative grip. But if we believed transformation were possible, we could lean into that potential for change. We could imagine a different future for our kids as the timeline of restoration continued into the next generation.

Years later, Jon wrote the lyric "Let's *not* be our parents." And we would add, let's *be* completely new people as parents. This hope became a reliable compass for our family. It is grace, one new beginning after another.

Creating a New Family Map

Our family road maps are literally the neurological pathways created during our childhoods. A humorous example is that whenever Mark's mother would quickly raise her hand, even during polite conversation, all her kids would duck. They had been conditioned to anticipate her quick temper!

The human brain is adapting constantly to its environment, able to learn new survival skills until, with practice, they become embedded, automatic. These preset responses simplify our lives so we don't have to start from scratch each time we drive to work or tie our shoes. We recognize familiar faces, or learn how to converse with strangers, through repeated experiences.

It's a safe bet that many of our attitudes and actions as parents come from this hidden subconscious realm. We will naturally parent how we were parented. But sometimes our automatic reflexes are off. We anticipate dangers that are not present or repeat easy lines that are now hurtful or misunderstood. We avoid certain people or settings for reasons we can't explain. Prejudice is one glaring example.

It's easy to spot the defects of others, but we are often blind to our own. We don't recognize our own unique blend of our parents' influence because it isn't quite the same flavor.

I recall sitting in Jon's first-grade open house, listening to the effervescent teacher describe her classroom goals: "Of course, I will never use guilt to motivate these children," she explained. Then she added, "No one, not even a parent, should ever try to motivate a child by using guilt!"

It were as though a police helicopter had begun circling my soul, complete with searchlight and bullhorn, isolating the well-traveled roadway of moralistic fears. I was raised in a strict church that held only a big stick and no carrots. Was there ever *any* motivation without guilt? I was busted.

I began to recognize my own brand of subtle shaming, making my children feel bad about crossing lines rather than explaining the reasons for them. Yet I had used this twisted discipline without giving it a second thought because it was ingrained. I began to notice and apprehend this wounding habit.

We had polished many other knee-jerk reactions over two decades: using sarcasm to win, withdrawing, ignoring hurt, getting loud to be heard, and avoiding disappointment. Granted, these might have been winning strategies in childhood, or they were originally responses to pain we once thought effective. Now, most were causing pain in our current relationships, especially with our kids. But the turnaround could begin when we honestly spotted a hurtful pattern.

The easiest, most obvious change in our direction came by mutual agreement over where we *didn't* want to go:

- We both belonged to the TV-tray generation, yet we questioned the TV as the focal point for meals.
- We were required to dress differently for church out of respect, but we wanted our kids to feel at home in God's house.
- Feelings in both of our childhood homes were largely ignored or rarely shared, but we wanted open, authentic conversations.

- God was a moral construct in our religious upbringing, so we would encourage our kids to have a relevant, warm relationship instead.
- We experienced some generational segregation, so we wanted our kids included in adult activities whenever possible.

Thankfully, we can use any liabilities for our family's future good, turning weaknesses into strengths.

Clear guidance also came by building on the assets of each of our families:

- My family made a sacrament out of holiday meals, thoughtfully planned and celebrated. But I also enjoyed the spontaneous informality of Mark's family, where the guests were the focus, not the flowered centerpiece.
- Mark learned the skill of listening from my quiet family, while I was encouraged to speak more openly about my opinions.
- Both families set the bar high on faithfulness and integrity, and we wanted to follow their inspiring examples.
- Our families enjoyed simply being together, on vacations or at regular meals, so we learned to keep this rhythm in our home.

Our own childhood experiences can be some of our best preparations for parenting. As we realistically accept our stories, we can learn from both the strengths and the weaknesses of our upbringing. That sifted history can provide a very reliable map for a new family.

Drawing a New Map

All families can be mapped or described in various ways:

- How is the family organized?
- Who's in charge?
- How do we communicate with each other?
- Are we generally close or distant?
- Are we flexible or rigid?

Talking together about family dynamics helps to pinpoint the conflicts between various areas in tension. Not surprisingly, this family equilibrium may go back several generations. And understanding the patterns and expectations can greatly impact our quality of life for the better.[2]

As we have this sensitive ongoing dialogue about our histories, it's vital to have a few golden rules for the road. It's too simplistic to scapegoat one person or tribe with all our pitfalls. We want to be very careful not to insult each other's family, parents, or siblings. We all can be realistic without being judgmental, which is a delicate balance. But negative stereotypes can cause damage to our present relationships. Instead, being able to forgive and release anyone who has hurt us is critical to moving on in our new family. Anything less will drag the past wounds into our existing home.

Creating a new family map is never without a struggle, like pulling our tires out of a ditch, again and again. It takes a long time and much earthmoving to form a new interstate. But it is possible.

We naturally fight for what we know. Familiar and family live under the same roof. But what is familiar is not always best for the home. It takes courage, honesty, and persistence to create a new family map. We need to allow space to change, enough air to grow, and to keep the lid on our unrealistic expectations, which can be quite flammable. I'll admit, many of the changes I fought the most were the best for us in the end.

My family plotted out menus a week in advance. Writing events on a calendar engraved them in stone. We always went for a Sunday drive. We made reservations at motels on vacation.

Mark's family breathed spontaneity like oxygen that kept them alive. They drove till they were tired and ate when they got hungry, wherever they happened to be. Every day was unique.

Now I am more spontaneous than Mark.

/// **IT'S ALMOST INTOXICATING TO REALIZE THAT ALL THINGS CAN BECOME NEW.** /// How we speak, our tone of voice, how we listen or argue, how we play, as well as our attitudes toward hard work—all can be made new.

Your History Matters

The structure of anything is critical. *Vasa* was a Swedish warship built from 1626–1628. The king of Sweden, Gustavus Adolphus, ordered the ship specifically for war. It was lavishly decorated to symbolize the king's powerful ambitions. But the ship floundered and sank after sailing only fourteen hundred yards into her maiden voyage on August 10, 1628.[3]

Vasa was dangerously unstable because of too much weight in the upper structure of the hull. It lacked ballast and a deep-enough keel to balance the weight. Despite this lack of stability, she was sent out to sea because the king was in a hurry and could not be bothered. It met a strong wind, and the ship sank before it had a chance to sail.

Many relationships do the same. In haste and ceremony, we embark on our voyages without much thought for stability but have unsafe structural problems that endanger our future together. We are too hurried and confident to notice what lies below the surface, to check our balances, if our keels are deep enough to support the added weight.

If we want our ships to sail well in all conditions for decades, we need to talk openly about how everyone in each of our families connects, how our past influences our present, and monitor our balance to make sure we don't sink. We can build and rebuild our relationships to last a lifetime.

Questions

What are some of the characteristics of how you were parented?

Have you spotted any of these traits or patterns in your own parenting style?

How might you want to change that road map in your own family? What do you want to preserve?

Chapter 3
I ENJOY YOU
Rewriting "Cat's in the Cradle"

BY MARK

And the cat's in the cradle and the silver spoon
Little boy blue and the man in the moon
When you comin' home, son?
I don't know when, but we'll get together then, Dad
You know we'll have a good time then.
—Harry Chapin, "Cat's in the Cradle"

The night roar of LA freeway traffic was a sharp contrast to the painful silence inside our car as we drove the two long hours home from Huntington Beach. A casual remark by our dinner host had inadvertently unearthed buried feelings in me toward God. Exiting the freeway, we made our ascent up the mountain—one vertical mile to our mountain cabin. Climbing into the evergreen darkness brought us no closer to heaven. Jan sensed my growing angst.

After we arrived home, the quiet followed us inside as we tucked in our sleeping three- and five-year-olds at almost midnight. I walked downstairs, lit a fire, and whispered to Jan, "Get some sleep." I wanted space to work through this undefined turmoil. Jan stubbornly countered that she would stay up too.

Some molten eruption was brewing—not depression, fear, or loneliness, but something deeper. Jan sat like a patient midwife while I stared into the rising smoke of red embers. I wrestled internally like Jacob did with the angel. Finally, I cracked the silence. I spoke to God.

To my surprise, anger and tears exploded with words that shocked me. Without logic, I heard myself cry to God, "Stop driving me.… With You, it's never enough.… I'm exhausted, yet You still want more!" As Jan gently patted my back, I sobbed and wondered, *Am I having a breakdown?*

Yet I knew my compulsion to achieve came from within. I was driving myself but projecting it onto God. I thought, *Surely God will strike me with lightning after such accusations.*

Again silent, drained of emotion, I waited. Then softly, an answer came. I knew the words didn't originate in my mind because they weren't in my vocabulary. This was a sentence I'd never heard and a theology I had not known. Seismically, three words shook the core of my being.

"I enjoy you."

Wiping the tears, I let the phrase settle quietly into my soul. Like unwrapping a gift, I began to parse the sentence. The "I," first-person singular, was obviously God. He was the subject initiating the delight. "Enjoy" was the verb in present tense, not the past, but now. And "you," the object of His joy, was me! Could this be true?

"I, God, personally delight in and enjoy being with you!"

A Revelation

I understood the doctrine of grace—at least I thought I did. I had heard preachers (myself included) recite, "God accepts you just the way you are." But "I enjoy you" was different. God's acceptance is a lifesaving, judicial truth; we are forgiven. But merely to accept someone does not convey desire or delight. So in my mind, God's acceptance was just a notch above tolerance: God in His grace *permits* us to come into His presence and heaven. But to *enjoy* someone indicates forward motion from God that expresses intentional and personal delight.

/// GOD'S CREATING, CHOOSING, AND REDEEMING US ALL POINT TO THIS: HE DELIGHTS IN US! /// "I enjoy you" means that God wants to be with us, now and always. Like a father or mother playing with his or her toddler, God enjoys simply being together.

He was not driving me like an angry disappointed father. Yes, God gave me a calling and wanted to use me, but He is not a utilitarian being who wants us only for what we can accomplish for Him. He wants to grab coffee and do life together.

Still, I had my doubts: *Am I a heretic? Are these thoughts just a humanistic hangover? Carl Rogers might agree with this insight, but would God?*

I mentally scanned the Bible for passages that would validate this idea. Then I found it: "He will take great delight in you [and] rejoice over you with singing" (Zeph. 3:17). The prophet went further to imagine God dancing and singing with joy over His redeemed people.

Then I remembered God walking in the cool of the day with the first couple, and David, the "apple of God's eye," and Psalm 139 where God's thoughts toward us were more than the sands of the sea. But ultimately, I wondered if God's loving thoughts were only to fulfill His saving agenda. Or could His thoughts of love also be personal because He wanted to be with us?

I couldn't recall hearing this message about God's pure delight, ever. I knew God was a good, loving Creator with an agenda: redeeming this world. But to realize God identified each of us on that crowded globe as a source of joy was a transforming revelation.

Enjoyment Doesn't Come Easy

Realizing that God enjoyed me didn't instantly fix my ingrained habits of performance. Accepting this intimate delight was initially foreign and uncomfortable. It was too personal, a letting go of the familiar resourcefulness to grab hold of a new vulnerability.

My achieving posture was watered partially by my engineer father, who would only nod at my report card of As and Bs, then teasingly ask, "Why weren't they A+s?" This really meant, "I'm proud of you." He, of course, was the product of his parents. Let the games begin.

We are a society that keeps score. Performance-based living, even in a culture of grace, is epidemic. Raised to be the best, it's hard not to view God as cracking the whip. My parents bragged about my accomplishments, but our free time together was often limited and centered on tasks.

In *Your God Is Too Small*, J. B. Phillips warned that we dare not construct a "100 percent God."[1] As our character is shaped, God desires maturity, not neurotic perfectionism. God actually wants to deliver us from Planet Performance. Just like the father of the prodigal son, He wants to throw a party of raw grace.

Now God's enjoyment was in my blood. I wanted God's pleasure reflected in everything—especially parenting. This "I enjoy you" had to be felt by my own two sons now that I had tasted God's pleasure.

The Cats in Our Own Cradles

When Jon was born, I was finishing grad school and working two jobs, amounting to an eighty-hour workweek. I tried to do it all, but something had to give because the family was getting crumbs. Baby Jon saw little of his daddy for the first few months of his life.

One sleepy night, rocking Jon as he snacked on his 2:00 a.m. bottle, I was jolted by a sudden question: What if you save five thousand people but lose your own son? The answer to this probing thought was obvious. I did not want to be that guy who was so busy helping others that he had no time for his own children.

Harry Chapin's folk song of 1974 immortalized the sad role reversal of an ignored child growing up to be just like his dad, whom he now ignores. My generation was raised in cat's-in-the-cradle families, of the song's era. My father was a great provider and example in many ways, but personal time did not come easy or often. I remember asking my dad several times to shoot hoops or to play catch while he relaxed on the couch watching Saturday sports on TV. After pausing, he would tell me to come back in a little while, which I always did. Then predictably, he would respond, "I guess not right now." I noticed my older brother had quit asking, and after a few attempts, I also gave up. But this was normal fatherhood. He was like all the other couch dads on our block.

Was I going to be just like those fathers? I was certainly at a crossroads. Our baby was challenging me to be a different parent. Would I learn and change or repeat the habits of my dad's generation? Would I be a father who was emotionally absent or truly be present for my child? The answer could be tangibly measurable by a limited commodity: time.

I made drastic changes in my schedule after counting the cost. Love is costly, but the price for losing touch with my sons was much too high. I could buy back the lost moments when my son was tiny, but I would not have this option when he was grown. To rewrite the lyric and my story, I wanted to have a good time *now*.

Love Is Spelled T-I-M-E

Love is wildly popular, in conversations and songs. Everyone believes in love, at least we think so. But believing is not the problem. It's the doing.

How is love best described? Self-sacrifice might be the highest definition: "Greater love has no one than this: to lay down one's life for one's friends" (John 15:13). This thankfully gets us past warm feelings to costly actions. Dying for someone we love is the ultimate proof. What loving parent wouldn't give his or her life for a child?

But as we break that life down into smaller increments, it is simply made up of time: minutes, hours, days, and years. We may be ready to sacrifice blood for our beloveds in times of crises, but not always our precious day-to-day time. We can imagine ourselves as the parent hero in some big screen moment, but can we also play a bit part in the daily routine?

Ultimately, love is spelled T-I-M-E.

/// **TIME IS THE CURRENCY OF ALL RELATIONSHIPS.** /// It's precious because we all get only twenty-four hours per day. Once we spend an hour, we can't recapture it—it's gone forever. If we spend an hour or two with our children, we can't spend those same hours on anything else. The hour is sacrificed for them. It's gone.

Doing the math, 2 hours a day equals 14 hours a week, about 56 hours a month, which becomes 730 hours a year. Spread over 20 years, this means 608 full days, or almost two years of our lives.

But it takes more than two hours a day to raise children. A grade school child requires an hour in the morning, an hour at supper, and at least an hour of shuttling and getting ready for bed. Now include homework, sports, practices, special needs, and extracurricular activities, and the average grade school child demands three to five hours a day. This isn't even quality time; it's just busy time.

An infant and toddler demand even more. Those early years are front-loaded with urgencies. The teens through the twenties have back-loaded demands in worry alone, over friends, dating, college or career, and other almost-adult choices. Going from worry and hurry to a slower "hang" time is costly.

Time, time, time is the high price of a loving parent, but who has time? Jan and I believed that if we invested our time heavily in our kids while young, we would give them a growing deposit from which to draw when they were older. It was a calculated risk we were willing to take.

Love Tank

Jon was a handful. He was a nine-pound eating, drinking, gregarious blond Viking who landed on our shores and instantly pillaged our tidy little village. Our lives had been organized and disciplined, with time for quiet, study, exercise, and friends, all plotted on a pie chart. Jon wonderfully blew up our world order.

But we were armed and ready, with parenting books of the '70s, which were largely a reaction to the freethinking books of the '60s. Discipline was in vogue again. Like minutemen waiting for the British at Concord, we felt equipped to discipline our new cherub, should he rebel.

But before our second child, Tim, was born, we realized we were losing the war. The hammer of enforcement is only one tool in a parent's belt, and it wasn't working for us. Jon was in charge; we were reacting and he was actually raising us.

Then we stumbled on a book that altered our approach: *How to Really Love Your Child* by D. Ross Campbell. Campbell imagined in every child a capacity for emotional well-being, which he called a love tank.[2] A child who feels loved is generally well behaved. But when the love tank is empty, the child becomes unruly. Children act out their need for love.

Parents, who obviously love their children, don't always know each child's love language. We don't know how to fill the tank. Like linguists acquiring a new language, parents must learn to communicate love to their children in a way they understand, love that is not just expressed in words. For Jan and me, it translated into our kids' needs for eye contact, touch, and quality time.

Eyes. Touch. Time. We began to listen to Jon and Tim with our eyes, communicating their value. We intentionally held or touched them when we spoke. We lengthened our focused time with play and reading. Becoming fluent in this new love language worked magically. But what our kids loved the most combined all three loving expressions: wrestling.

Every day after work, from the moment I walked through the door, we would tumble around on the carpet. Sometimes for only half an hour; other times for an hour and a half. Their love tanks were huge, but our parenting assignment each day was to fill those tanks. Then we noticed: rarely was there a serious discipline problem on a full tank.

We grew close because we enjoyed being together. This is an axiom for all relationships: it's hard to like someone if you don't spend much time with that person. Although we continued to wrestle and read, the quality time adapted and changed as our kids grew up. We played catch, went for bike rides, kicked a soccer ball, played music, and now surf together. This bond continues to grow. The love language has shifted, but the communication lives on. More than ever, we genuinely enjoy our kids.

Never Say No

Where do two-year-olds learn the defiant no? Behavioral science insists toddlers are individuating themselves as they move through an important developmental stage. That said, an added reason is possible: they learn this word from us. As parents frequently use the word in those early years, the child realizes its power. They can hardly wait to use *that* word—*no*!

But sadly, adults may never stop using the word. We might say no to playing tag or to the request to build a fort or read a story (that we have read many times). We may soften the no with "Not now," but children quickly learn that next time may never come and, like I did, quit asking.

Of course, children can make unhealthy demands or cry for attention to test us. This is a "mistaken goal," according to Dr. Rudolf Dreikurs, because the child insists on being the center of attention.[3] But often such insecurity arises from an absence of focused time with the parent. We must leave margins for play in our efficient lives.

Be available to accept your child's invitations. Jan and I still live by this motto: Never say no. When our sons or grandchildren ask us to climb a tree, build a sand castle, go for breakfast, or paddle into dark, frigid, windblown waves, the answer is always yes. /// **GOD IS ONE BIG *YES* FOR US, AND WE WANT TO PAY IT FORWARD TO OUR OWN KIDS.** ///

This is how we rewrite "Cat's in the Cradle": "Never Say *No*."

The Incarnation for Parents: It's Cool in the Pool

If God truly enjoys us, then our delight in our children can mirror heaven's. We can actively share in their joy each day, step by step, or choose to be absent from their lives except for great accomplishments.

Just as Jesus fully entered our human experience, we parents can jump into our children's wonder-filled world.

My mom, Doreen, was the classiest grandmother I have ever known. In the 1980s, she drove a cream 450 SL Mercedes convertible around Southern California, always dressed fashionably, with acrylic nails and well-styled frosted hair. But Doreen never fit into the pretentious OC mold, and we loved her for being both classy and crazy, in the very best sense. "Wild Thing," by the Troggs, was the sound track for her life.

It was Thanksgiving Day in Newport Beach, but the temperature felt more like the Fourth of July. Doreen had been slicing, baking, stirring, and washing dishes since 6:00 a.m. She served her food according to her personality: in an open house, buffet style on casual paper plates to dozens of relatives and friends of relatives who kept arriving.

It must have been stifling in that kitchen, because most of the party moved outside onto the deck. Several generations were sweating it out on lounge chairs or patio furniture as they consumed their turkey. But all the grandkids were having the best celebration, jumping in and out of the pool in the backyard.

Around 3:00 p.m., Grandma Doey, as she was called, decided to resign her post behind the sink. She took off her gravy-soaked apron and, with the confident swagger of a burlesque dancer, made her exit from the kitchen. She grabbed a damp beach towel, twirled it over her head, and without a word, approached the pool. Then, with a sly grin as if to say, "Watch this," she kicked off her high heels and leaped into the pool, joining the kids. Her perfectly styled hairdo, pearls, and elegant dress were all baptized in a Thanksgiving expression we will never forget.

Jon was underwater when he caught sight of his grandmother, fully clothed, joining him at the bottom of the pool. He remembers thinking, *Hey, there's Grandma*, but kept swimming because that was just the sort of behavior he had come to expect from an elder so young at heart.

We all realized the brilliance of that instant cool down, and like lemmings, we followed Doreen's example, splashing into the water, leaving our uneaten plates of food in the sun. We were actually following our kids who were wisely already submerged. Why were we protecting our outfits and appearances and turkey traditions when we could have fun and stay cool? "Wild Thing" became our theme song too.

This is what is required for parents to fully engage in relationship with their children. We must at times leave behind our serious adult business and jump into the fun sensibility of being a child in their time and space. Not to be childish, but childlike in the wonder, honesty, and ability to play. When we cross this border from adult to child, it communicates loudly that we are interested in them.

Do we expect our young children to join us in the hot kitchen, perusing recipes and scrubbing pans? Sometimes. But can we also look out the window and find a better time for both of us in what they are already doing? Can we be inconvenienced to freely jump feet first into their world?

Of course, this is what God did when He arrived in Bethlehem as a helpless newborn. For three short decades, He swam in our pool, drenched in humanity. Now we can never say that God does not know, feel, or understand our lives, because He chose to share our whole experience on earth. Jesus did not simply watch us from a safe distance. He jumped right in.

Returning the Favor

Not only can we plunge into our children's world of play, but we can allow them to enter our adult space. Like watercolors colliding on wet paper, sometimes there are happy accidents, when the sterile blue sky collides with a red fence post and creates a purple glow on the horizon. When we let young minds into our grown-up space, we can create something fresh and inspiring for both ages.

Jan and I included our kids in our daily routines whenever possible. We introduced them to key people at work. I explained my teaching process. Jan let them paint alongside her easel, and I let them ride as small passengers on my windsurfer. They helped Jan create grocery lists and picked out the items at the store. I took them to the lumberyard to select wood, then handed out small hammers. The possibilities are endless.

Of course we all fear becoming the tiger mom or perfectionist dad who rigidly plans to mold the child into the same career path or favorite hobby. Playing golf with Daddy or going to the office with Mommy can have a manipulative angle. Caution is needed when something as large as an adult collides with someone as small and sensitive as a child. The invitation to join us in our world is simply for authentic relationship.

The Art of Being

Several years ago, we stood in awe at the base of Michelangelo's towering statue of David in Florence, Italy. The apostle Paul declared that we are God's *masterpiece* (Eph. 2:10 NLT). The term is *poiema*, which means "poem" or "work of art." God wants to sculpt our lives with His love and truth, to creatively write His character on our hearts. This daily experience of transformation is the art of becoming who we are designed *to be*.

The art of parenting, however, often requires us to focus on *doing*. We attend school meetings and read health literature, then teach our kids to make beds, brush teeth, and clean toilets. But we must all become *who* God has created us to *be*. Personal transformation applies to kids too.

A wise president of our alma mater once told visiting parents, "Choose a college based on *who* you want your student to be, not based on *what* occupation you want for them." Our panoramic view as parents is not only of the microscopic details of what we want our children *doing* but especially of *who they are and will be*. It is their inner strength of character shining underneath—the *being*—that ultimately shapes their lives. We never want to lose sight of the *poiema* or poetry of God in our children. What we instill inside will eventually work its way outside.

A family friend has been a Young Life leader for over two decades, so he holds a front-row seat on the unfolding stories of many kids. He has tracked them from awkward adolescence through the independent early thirties. Some kids found the shift from childhood to adulthood painfully difficult, while others landed on their feet quite smoothly.

When I asked what he felt was the biggest factor in growing up gracefully, without hesitation he replied, "The kids who had parents who genuinely enjoyed them."

These are the moms and dads whose faces light up when they talk about their children or when they spot their kids in crowds. They break into wide grins—not grimaces. Without a doubt, a parent's pleasure—or displeasure—is detectable to kids. It may not be the only reason a child grows up well, but it is certainly a viable contender.

Maybe this delight is birthed naturally inside moms or dads when they first hold their infant, but what happens when the baby fusses at 3:00 a.m. or develops a temper or refuses to clean a room? We're irritated, exhausted, and longing for peace. But can there be a transcending joy that exists outside of our child's ability to be lovable? Thankfully, there is such a joy.

"I enjoy you" can become a friendly octopus, with arms reaching in all directions. It helped me communicate not only my joy for my kids but also that God enjoyed them and they could celebrate His delight-full purpose. It gave them courageous hearts, allowing them to take risks and say yes to new challenges. It helped them appreciate and enjoy other people. I often said, "I love who you are," and I still mean it.

We are shaped by our closest relationships. Our personalities rub off on each other as we practice new traits through time spent together. During these critical close encounters, our children observe and absorb who we are. This brings the question back to us: Do we enjoy our children? More importantly, do we know the delight of God's love for us so we might purely enjoy our children for who they are?

Questions

How comfortable are you with the realization that God enjoys you? Explain.

Do you genuinely enjoy your child? What are some things that give you delight?

How could you enter into your child's playful world more freely?

What would it look like to invite your child into your world?

Chapter 4

MATCHING T-SHIRTS

Family Values

BY JAN

All happy families resemble each other; each
unhappy family is unhappy in its own way.
—Leo Tolstoy, *Anna Karenina*

Mark's great-grandparents migrated west by covered wagon in 1887 to explore the open space. When our family of four made a reverse leap "eastward ho" from California in 1982, we wanted to create our own story. Getting there would be part of our adventure. We drew an indirect route that included many famous sites in the United States: Las Vegas; the Great Salt Lake; Cody, Wyoming; Niagara Falls; and of course Mount Rushmore, which we reached after five days on the road.

Our covered wagon was a yellow four-wheel-drive Subaru packed with anything we might need on our eight-day journey. When we parked our station wagon in the shadow of those giant stone presidents, we crawled out looking like a homeless family—which we were.

There were four of us and four of them: Washington, Jefferson, Roosevelt, and Lincoln. Yep, there they were, looming large as we expected, just like all the pictures. But what we were not anticipating were all the matching tourists, family groups wearing identical T-shirts, dressed for reunion photographs. One by one, each clan took turns posing in front of the presidents, rows of cousins and aunts, babies and grandparents, smiling beneath the silent leaders. Perhaps they hoped that backdrop of greatness would inspire future generations to identify with those immortalized in stone.

But the T-shirts that expressed each family's personality would tell the real story of each tribe. Beneath the obvious physical similarities of red hair, stocky build, or prominent nose, there lay a shared emotional, social, and relational code.

Each family has a distinct culture. Our kids inherit not only our brown eyes or freckled skin but also our values. This social DNA begins to clothe each child's soul from birth like a matching T-shirt inscribed with his or her family motto. It's not just *what* we do or say but also *how* and *why* that ultimately determine who we, and our kids, become. Our values color the *way* we do everything.

Unpacking a Red Suitcase

Identifying our particular values is like finding separate clouds in the fog—we are so saturated by their presence, they're hard to spot. But our children have a way of revealing what is most precious to us.

One morning, my three-year-old grandson said wistfully, "What I would really like is a trophy." Then I remembered: out of sight, in the farthest corner of a crawl space above our cluttered garage, was a grade-school-through-college stash of our sons' trophies, hidden in a worn suitcase. It was a faded red treasure chest full of shiny gold and silver figurines, some with marble bases, others attached to solid dark wood. There were awards for soccer, surfing, tennis, baseball, and academic contests. All were haphazardly wrapped, so each unveiling felt like a Christmas surprise.

I wasn't sure why my grandson wanted a trophy, but he probably had witnessed some ceremony and understood these were important things. Indeed. Why else would I have saved them for over a decade?

/// **WHAT WE PRIZE IS OFTEN HIDDEN, BUT LITTLE HANDS AND HEARTS BRING IT TO LIGHT.** /// We quickly discovered through our kids the naked truth, that what we proudly said was most vitally important was often not how we voted with our time and energy.

It's not our rhetoric but our reactions that expose what we actually value. And these silent trophies, unpacked by our young, continuously, incrementally, undeniably shape us—and our kids.

Red Light, Green Light

Our core values are the red lights and green lights that control our stops and starts. They create the style or personality of our lives. Every family has a collection of favorites, but they go largely unnoticed until a conflict or decision arises.

This dynamic was clear even before we had our first child. We prepared to move into a larger apartment in Pasadena when I was seven months pregnant, allowing Mark to finish his last year of grad school. We were conveniently close to our chosen obstetrician and a reputable hospital. We retained our close-knit community of friends, who were also starting families. Then a phone call one night rattled our impeccable plan.

"Would you like to move to Lake Arrowhead and teach in the Bible school starting next month?"

Mark's initial response was predictable, spoken like a first-time father guarding his young: "No, that is not what we want to do at this time." He gave all the right reasons: Jan near delivery, our deposit on the apartment, and Mark needing to finish school.

But I overheard the conversation from the next room, and something stirred inside, a voice that said we should not be so quick to walk past this open door. I entered the room and said softly, "Let's stay open and at least pray about this." When a first-time mother, seven months pregnant, is willing to move her nest, there must be hidden values at stake, which Jon was unwrapping even before birth.

The next day, I shared our dilemma with older friends who had been missionaries in China and birthed at least one child in a concentration camp.

"You sound like a couple of old ladies," the wife teased. How could we miss such a great opportunity to serve others because we wanted to play safe and not adjust our plans?

We were facing a clash of family values, each side shouting why this was the best choice: security versus faith; predictability versus adventure; responsibility versus obedience to a call.

This is our lifelong challenge as parents. Deciding what matters most is like a beauty pageant: There are no ugly faces, and we are often choosing between good and good. All are attractive options (usually).

We moved to Lake Arrowhead.

Our strongest desires surfaced through that early struggle that helped define our family. Landing in the mountains was not simply a geographical choice. That decision set a course that was often challenged but became a regular pattern. We would embrace change and the unknown as a family if we believed we were following God's good call.

This also explains why we moved our family again, six years later, leaving that serene mountain community for the unfamiliar East Coast. It was more than a restless call of the wild; it was the inner call of what was most important to all of us.

The Mundane Can Reveal What Matters Most

Better a dry crust with peace and quiet than
a house full of feasting, with strife.
—Proverbs 17:1

Our core DNA can also surface through routine events. Even meals can be a proving ground for family values. We recently ate lunch at an upscale restaurant, and I noticed a boy of about eight at the next table. I was struck by how anxiously he ate, mentioning multiple times that he was *not* going to spill a thing on his new sweater. What had this nervous son learned about his family's values? Maintaining a clean appearance trumps enjoying a meal together?

On Sundays, my family ate formally at my grandparents' dining room table, set with fine china, stemware, and linen. Hands were held in silence while my grandfather blessed the meal with eyes closed in a sacred hush. Hungry eaters waited to lift a fork until the last person was served and asked "May I please be excused?" when plates were cleared. After dessert, everyone migrated to the sunroom to watch the latest episode of *Gunsmoke*.

But when my family moved to California, the scene changed dramatically. My parents were often dieting, my sister and I became teenagers, my dad's job required later hours, and my mom went back to work as an emergency room RN. We discovered TV trays, and we no longer sat facing each other but chose to be entertained by Ed Sullivan. Even when gathered at the table, the TV was always on, so conversation was minimal.

Mark, on the other hand, grew up a third-generation Californian. Formality was unheard of, and most feasts were served on paper plates with seating wherever you could find a chair or space on the floor. The best conversations took place in the large kitchen or on the backyard patio. It was never just the immediate family, but other relatives and friends would cruise in and out, adding to the spontaneous mood. The decibel levels were high, and so was the fun.

Our mealtimes and other routines expose various homegrown values that are subject to change. Maybe none of these expressions are better than others, but they are very distinct and lead to completely different places. Those mealtimes are not just about furnishing people with calories. The shopping list of groceries prior to a feast is not as significant as the way we serve the food.

In the same way, finding my values is more than writing a to-do list each day. It even goes beyond determining what I love most; it's *how* I love those people, dreams, objects, or ideals. It's not just what I say, but how I say it; not what I accomplish, but how I get the job done. What matters most is revealed by how I actually live.

Inside the family van on a Sunday morning drive to church can be more insightful than the sermon, with parents not speaking, or yelling at the kids because they've made them late—again! What does this unhappy scene actually say about what matters most? Our love for God and one another takes a backseat to keeping up appearances and being on time? Or maybe we slept in and guilt was really driving us to church? Our media is always the message.

Ideally, our values integrate our thoughts, emotions, and actions: what we believe, how we feel, and what we do. But often we're divided and our actions contradict our gut responses—or what we say we believe does not resonate with us emotionally or with our calendars.

I can say that I value good health, but if I grab a handful of Peanut M&M's for breakfast and skip the morning gym, what do I really want? A moment's ecstasy for the taste buds and sleeping in? An authentic value gets my attention and my vote in the daily parade of options.

Parents have a gravitational pull on their children, not with words, but in their lifestyle. We can't sell our kids on broccoli if we won't touch it ourselves or encourage good books if we are non-readers. /// AS PARENTS, WE CAN RATTLE OFF IDEALS ABOUT WHO WE WANT OUR KIDS TO BE, BUT OUR DAILY CHOICES MAY BE WORKING AGAINST THOSE ASPIRATIONS. /// Our emotional reactions will push them in the opposite direction. As someone wisely said, "It's not what you say but how you make a child feel that counts."

Parents have a time-sensitive opportunity to combine what we truly want and believe with what we actually do, especially because kids are adept at revealing the gaps. Mark and I jumped into caring for people at the same time we began our family. At twenty-four years, I was catapulted into helping folks often three times my age, so I felt apologetic about the quality of my care. I was often driven by the value of approval rather than setting realistic expectations that guarded my mommy time. Sure, I was physically present, but I was often distracted in those early years by the applause or lack thereof. The awareness that I was doing more but enjoying everything else less caused me eventually to set saner limits and delegate more. I was the only mom, but there were plenty of qualified personnel in God's house.

Being aware of our inconsistencies can be our first insight in the battle for a wholehearted family. We can stop and edit the mixed messages. How powerful would it be to send one clear message to our kids about what is worth living for?

Asking Better Questions

We can intentionally uncover our values by simply asking what matters most to us. What are our personal trophies? What qualities do we prize for our kids? Often parents can detect these values in each other more easily than in their own lives.

If we simply write down all the important things in our lives, we will quickly fill pages. But isolating what ranks in the top five or ten is complicated and never easy. Competing treasures wrestle for first place: I value simplicity, yet I hate to throw things away. I want time with my family but also to serve my community. We need one-on-one time with each child but also time alone with each other.

As parents, we wear many hats with competing roles. Early in our parenting journey, Mark and I struggled to find balance among increasingly complicated demands. In desperation, I ordered a popular audio course from FranklinCovey on how to manage time according to what mattered most, our values. Stephen Covey wrote, "Peace of mind comes when your life is in harmony with true principles and values and in no other way."[1]

We were certainly seeking peace as we juggled conflicting expectations as parents, relatives, coworkers, and friends.

So we carved out time to listen not only to the audio lessons but also to our own inner voices, sorting through our pile of commitments. This was the initial step, carving out time to consider time itself and how we were randomly spending our days. It became instantly clear: we gave most of our attention to urgencies, not essentials.

In *Tyranny of the Urgent*, Charles Hummel wrote, "When we stop long enough to think about it, we realize that our dilemma goes deeper than shortage of time; it is basically a problem of priorities."[2]

So what were our priorities? What really mattered most? We began simply by talking about cherished qualities that fueled our goals and dreams: authenticity, courage, humility, curiosity, kindness, creativity, patience, and even fun were included.

It felt like sifting the beach looking for gold. But through the daily necessity of choosing one thing over another, we grabbed some gems from the abundance of sand:

- Mark decided to stay home more nights than he was gone.
- We chucked formality for more barbecues with guests.
- I learned to make bread rather than buy it sliced. (Nothing smells better.)
- Many nights, we let our kids entertain company with magic shows rather than plan more sophisticated options.
- We took surf trips to unusual places, not just easy destinations.

Ultimately, all of our values were related to people, especially those closest to us. These treasures would hopefully encourage us to be fully human, to authentically love God and others well.

Doing What Matters Most

Identifying what's important is insightful stuff, especially when it coincides with our passions. But the real life change happens when we move our feet in the same direction. So we committed to a new habit: We established a magic moment at the beginning of each day to look at the bigger picture. Before urgencies steal the show, we could write in our schedule what mattered most, harnessing our thoughts, emotions, and actions.

We could not only look ahead twenty-four hours but also scrutinize the week, the month, even the whole year. Taking a long look changes our perspective on the present demanding minute, with seconds ticking.

Those big-picture moments gave us a higher-elevation view of the distant future, where we realized the relational rewards or the sad outcome if we neglected these non-emergency treasures. We could continue to live disintegrated lives, estranged from what we truly valued. Or we could fight against the gaps and reconcile what was most important with our schedule.

Surprisingly, we found our most deeply held values waiting patiently in a quiet side room. Growing intimacy, fostering creativity, indulging curiosity—none of these are hot fires that need immediate attention. We can speak endlessly of "someday I will do that" instead of today.

Not all values are created equal. Some are only expedient; others are life sustaining. In our grab-and-go culture, it's easy to settle for quick fixes that conveniently numb or easily please our children in the present but don't cultivate strong minds or deep souls. Parents need the wise advice of master gardeners: Plant today for the garden you want in a few years. Don't impatiently settle for instant fillers that will eventually choke the life out of your prized plants.

Family Mottoes

Mark's parents had Joshua 24:15 inscribed above their fireplace: "As for me and my house, we will serve the Lord." Every family has favorite expressions, similar to tribal chants, that proclaim our aspirations like that verse on the mantel. These are the billboards placed along our childhood journey that advertised our parents' values.

We especially need to question any inherited mottoes that are undermining our new family but still echoing in our halls. We can toss those sayings that don't suit our new home, like the clothes our family left on the East Coast when we moved back to sunny California. If we don't expel the ghosts, they will quietly control the family.

One of my repeated family phrases was "What would people think …?" which was often followed by a worst-case scenario of how I would offend some faceless mob. The underlying value was to please people at all costs.

Mark grew up in the opposite universe, where every point needed to be stated and hammered loudly. You were validated by being right: "Argue for argument's sake. Play the devil's advocate."

As we began our new home, we wanted to expel any toxic values that could steal the good land, like squatters. We often resisted to an extreme, with opposing mottoes: "You do not need to care about what other people think" or "It's good to have a different opinion." Sometimes, we just need to burn the old family T-shirts and screenprint some fresh slogans.

Time, Energy, and Money

Our unique family histories will simply be a compilation of our choices. Even our passivity or the reluctance to choose is a decision. Every book that sits on the shelves of our lives is there by choice, either ours or someone else's. If we allow a certain volume to take up space, that is also under our control. This ability to choose freely comes with every human package.

Two truth tellers for my values are my calendar and my finances. These two witnesses faithfully record my time, energy, and money. What matters most will always monopolize one or more of these areas.

My calendar reveals my actual priorities and any large chasms that exist between what I believe and feel is important and my daily choices. But my calendar can also be the best tool to shape the future by replacing my emergency responses with more intentional patterns.

It's true; humans are creatures of habit. We can't fatten our core values without creating routines that back up our passions. If we move the things we truly want to the front of the line on our crowded calendars, we can create better habits: Mark and I tried to block off Saturday mornings for family devotions; we penciled in one date a week; we budgeted for a yearly vacation; I continued to teach but tried to avoid meetings on Mark's days off; Mark stopped taking appointments in the evening.

Just as telling as the calendar, our material assets also describe what we love most. A credit card statement, a prized object, or what we hoard can expose our actual values.

We had just replaced the upstairs carpet in our bedrooms with an expensive, courageous off-white plush. After the furniture was replaced, Jon resumed painting a model car in his room. Predictably, his project's card table wobbled and an entire jar of model paint tipped and landed upside down in the center of his room, leaving a giant black dot on once-spotless white tufts.

I was horrified and felt sickened.

Jon felt even worse, saying, "Sorry, sorry, sorry," like a penitent prayer.

I then asked the obvious, incriminating (dumb parent) questions: "Don't you know this carpet is brand-new? What were you thinking? Where is the newspaper to protect the floor?"

I took a few deep breaths as I mopped up the paint with Jon. With the aid of a miraculous stain remover, most of the black enamel was rubbed to a faint gray. But beyond the carpet damage, I sensed that my angry reaction to this little emergency had left another impermeable stain on Jon's soul. My appreciation of expensive carpet had spilled onto my priceless child.

As I continued to blot the dark ooze, I managed to find words for what I actually believed. "It was, after all, an accident. Everyone makes mistakes, takes shortcuts. You are much more important than a perfectly white rug. Of course."

Our children force us to choose. They expose the wrestling in our hearts over many competing loves. Is the relationship more valuable than my well-ordered world? Do I value my child more than a piece of furniture, the new car, or my appearance? Is this person more important than perfection, or achievement, or convenience, or whatever else is boiling to the surface demanding attention?

Our actions do not lie, although we can grow accustomed to their droning voice, passively accepting our status quo. Or we can interrupt the empty chatter of daily demands, consumer striving, and false success and replace it with our own true voice. We can start acting out our values and let those real-time choices shape us and our kids.

A Little Child Shall Lead

Our kids need to realize their own power to choose a meaningful life. We wanted our sons to take responsibility for their own lives, of course. But beyond survival, we wanted them to learn the essential life skill of discernment, to sort through what others might value to instead discover what was important to them.

This is the essence of leadership, making up your own mind and bringing others with you. If their friends raved about a movie or described camping as boring or thought a teacher was strict, they didn't have to agree. Having an open dialogue to explore the possibilities was valued above quick dogmatic answers. We believe this fosters not only critical thinking but also honest relationships. We encouraged our kids to process their opinions out loud, to entertain many ideas without forcing an instant black-and-white conclusion. We could walk together through the tension of competing ideas.

Our kids also led us to have new perspectives and approach life differently. They not only unpacked our existing values, but they pressed us to forge new ones or dust off some long ignored. These reclaimed treasures were surprising and refreshing: the good of play, wonder, fantasy, and the imagination. Flashlight tag might not get the laundry folded or mail read, but it held a prime slot in our week.

We began to notice obvious patterns too, likely encouraged by having kids. We preferred organic to slick, casual above formal, original to predictable, curious over being experts, and we hoped always to choose people over perfection.

One afternoon a friend stopped by unexpectedly, so I apologized for the wreckage of toys as she stepped over blocks, a tricycle, and

Matchbox cars. I explained this newfound freedom of letting go of my high standards, to which she replied, "Yes, I can see that is true!"

As we became more aware of our personal values, we also began to identify what we longed for in our children. We especially wanted to build on their strengths. Our list for them was similar to our own, but theirs had different emphases as we imagined them growing into adults: responsibility, persistence, patience, and resilience, all qualities that would serve them well in an uneven world of imperfect people. Responsibility is a "continuum" that should naturally and gradually increase as the child ages.[3]

One giant value seemed to encompass all the others: being well-rounded. A wise friend shared that we do not know whether our children will sit with the poorest of the poor or at a king's table. But we wanted our kids to be comfortable in every setting, able to relate to all people. We wanted to raise kids who looked for the good in all things.

Being well-rounded included us parents, which meant that we *all* needed to stay curious, continually adding to our repertoire of experiences: watercolor classes, four wheeling, learning cross-country skiing or the ukulele. /// LIFE MUST BE INTERESTING TO FOSTER INTERESTING KIDS—AND PARENTS. ///

These values colored our walls and flavored our conversations in and out of our home. We had family nights of hilarious games and noisy music. We gave our kids piano lessons but didn't let them quit when they weren't in the mood to practice. They were encouraged to remain at the table, included in adult conversations. We designed tree forts and studied the night sky together. We told them they could be anything they wished and we would always be proud.

We wanted our practices to come from an intentional place: a growing awareness of what mattered most to us. This was our unique culture. Every family will have its own quirky personality and look different from ours. We get to design our own matching T-shirts. That's not just okay; it is the whole wonderful point. It's the beauty of combining individuals of all ages into the messy collage we call family. Just like our kids, no two are alike.

> *Family values are a little like family vacations—subject to changeable weather and remembered more fondly with the passage of time. Though it rained all week at the beach, it's often the momentary rainbows that we remember.*
> —Leslie Dreyfous, *New York Times*, October 25, 1992

Questions

What could have been a slogan on your childhood family T-shirt?

What slogan do you wish for your own family T-shirt?

What are some of the things that matter most to you?

What qualities do you want to encourage in your child?

Looking back over your week, how did you spend most of your time?

What was the best part of your week? The worst?

How can you intentionally make time for what is important?

For the artistic and less verbal, draw a family crest using symbols of what matters most.

Chapter 5

KNOCK OFF, BABY

Made in Our Image

BY MARK

Children are great imitators. So give them something great to imitate.
—Anonymous

I love dogs. It's their masters who bother me.

Our mountain home overlooked an evergreen canyon. It was beautifully scenic, but all noises in the valley traveled uphill. Noises such as barking dogs. Night after night.

Late one night, around 2:00 a.m., I was done. The dogs were going off. And once our neighbor's dogs started barking, other dogs joined the choir. Scenes from *101 Dalmatians* were invading our bedroom. Before long, I heard in the distance howling coyotes joining the canine chorus. Not a dog was sleeping, and neither was I.

Finally, I leaped to my feet to take manly authority over the animal kingdom. After marching across our bedroom and into the bathroom, without hesitation, I slid open the window, pressed my face against the screen, and yelled at the top of my lungs, *"Knock it off!"* To my surprise and wonder, the night fell silent. Even the dogs were terrified by the mysterious voice from on high.

Making sure the family was still asleep, I smugly returned to bed with a grin. No one knew that tonight I had taken command of the world—at least the pooch world.

The next day, the dogs were at it again. But before I could retest my powers, toddler Jon ran across his room, climbed up on the toilet with his chubby legs, slid open the window, and hollered, "Knock off, baby!"

I had a stunt double.

After I recovered from laughter, I was sobered by the realization that Jon had perfectly mimicked me. He had heard me last night and memorized my actions when I thought he had been fast asleep and unaware. For better or for worse, he was my copycat.

Our Children Reveal Who We Are

It takes courage to grow up and become who you really are.

—E. E. Cummings

As parents, we have a built-in advantage: our kids are hardwired to be like us. They enter our world with a wide-open trust and admiration for the ones who created them. It sounds so simple—all we have to do is be ourselves, and they will follow. But that is both good news and bad news. It evokes the question, How many of me do I want on this planet? Two? Three? Or more?

/// **IF WE WANT AN HONEST LOOK AT OURSELVES, WE CAN WATCH OUR KIDS.** /// They are becoming us. Not exact replicas, but the similarities can be startling. Our children do us a favor: they shine flashlights into our souls. When we become aware of a bad habit or inadequacy, we have the opportunity to change. Children create that opportunity.

This means both parent and child get to grow up together. When meeting a family with older teens, I often say, "You've done a good job raising your parents." Some kids knowingly respond, "It hasn't always been easy." Growing up is challenging at any age.

This is the ongoing question for me: Am I still growing up? Or have I gotten stuck on some immature plateau, driven by fear or shrunk by cynicism or simply being lazily bored? Do I realize that my life matters, not only to me, but also to my family and innumerable others? Both the good and the bad are multiplying.

As toddler Jon's imitation demonstrated, our example is potent whether we intend it or not. It can be as innocuous as our loathing squash, or enjoying rap and disdaining opera, or the love of cats and fear of spiders. But our examples can also be life altering: authenticity, a compassion for the elderly, a critical attitude, our willingness to serve, or the reticence to try something new. Our children will digest all these lessons and regurgitate them in new forms. Knowing that our personal aversions and attractions will influence our kids means the primary task for parents is to raise *us*.

So another quick question might be: How would I want my kids to handle this situation—and how can I be that example? What do I do when someone snags my parking place, or we have unplanned expenses, or someone drops by unexpectedly as we're sitting down for dinner? The arrival of children forces the issue of our own transformation. That's why we must grow up first—and fast.

Following the Leader

From birth, we begin to play follow-the-leader. Children learn almost everything by imitation: initial sounds, facial expressions, language, walking, even how to use a smartphone before they turn two. They are excellent students, picking up the subtlest cues from their primary teachers, parents. They discover their own unique selves by trying on ours for size. Without need of copyright permission, our children are stealing our identities.

This lesson was brought home when we found a lost duckling, whom we named Spud Web. We lived near water in Hampton Roads, Virginia, so it was not uncommon to see ducks waddling along the gutter in our neighborhood after rain. One day we saw a mother with ducklings foraging in front of our house, but the following day, a forlorn duckling was waddling alone. We rescued it from the street and placed it in a cardboard box while we scoured the neighborhood for the missing mother.

We gave Spud rations, placed his box near my desk while I worked, and continued to look for his mother. Initially, Spud sat intently looking up at me, but soon, wanting nurture, he began to peep incessantly for attention. Spud's demands became so constant, I draped a hand towel on my shoulder and gave him this perch. I became Spud's permanent nest.

Then I had an alarming realization: Spud was bonding to me. I had become his mother duck—yikes!

The next day we took Spud to a bird refuge where he processed the hard reality that his mother had abandoned him. And he was really a duck, not a computer programmer. Back in his element, he eventually accepted that lifestyle. Thankfully, we could reverse the human imprint.

In the same way, children are incredibly impressionable as well as pliable. When Tim was almost four, Jan needed extra effort to lift her growing son into her arms.

"You are solid!" she remarked.

"No I'm not," he challenged. "I can still turn my head—see?" And he demonstrated. This is a built-in grace for parents: A child's character is not yet solidified, but moldable. Our early poor examples can be reshaped, just as Spud was reprogrammed, and even as we continue to change ourselves.

This sounds a bit daunting, but it is equally thrilling. The assignment is simply to be with our kids in the unfolding stories of our lives. For me, it was a second childhood, an opportunity to grow up with them. Even in my mistakes, I could model how God's "compassions never fail. They are new every morning" (Lam. 3:22–23). And what a joy to realize we are not alone on this journey toward maturity.

Created in Our Image

Actions speak louder than words but not nearly as often.
—Mark Twain

The saying "Do as I say, not as I do" just isn't realistic. We watch and do, over and over. We learn how to set the table, brush our teeth, react to danger, express our love, and carry a conversation all by observation. This is the wild and dangerous power of example, like stones thrown into a pond whose ripples intersect and overlap with others. Also called the butterfly effect, the flap of a slight wing can alter life on another continent.

Imitation is both implied and explicitly taught in Scripture. It is implied in Jesus's inviting the disciples to "come and see" and watch His life closely for three years. Then Paul used the term *mimeotai*, which means "imitate" or "mimic": "Be imitators of God, as beloved children" (Eph. 5:1 NASB). He referenced children because mimicking is natural for them.

The grandest opportunity for imitation, however, happened at creation when God made humans in His image:

> Then God said, "Let us make mankind in our image, in our likeness, so that they may rule over the fish in the sea and the birds in the sky, over the livestock and all the wild animals, and over all the creatures that move along the ground."
>
> So God created mankind in his own image, in the image of God he created them; male and female he created them. (Gen. 1:26–27)

God made us to resemble Him—to mirror His image—to the whole world. Perhaps this is why humans naturally mimic: it enables us to reflect the nature of God.

Creating our own offspring continues this amazing purpose; it multiplies God's face. As soon as each son was born, we studied his features to find some family resemblance. Jon had his grandmother's blond hair and blue eyes. Tim had my dad's brown eyes and hair. But our God resemblance is not about physical characteristics; it's about character. We are created to express God's incredible nature, His love and truth, His generosity and patience and wisdom.

So our parenting purpose is rooted in God's original brilliant design. We are created in His image to mimic God to others. Then we create our own children, who are expressions of that same life (Gen. 5:3; 9:6). We are privileged to pass on the nature of God through our unique humanity to each new generation.

A child's ability to mimic begins at birth. The newborn's eyes are able to focus the exact distance to the mother's face. As babies feed, they discover themselves in reference to the parents holding them.

James E. Loder wrote, "Children seem uniquely endowed with a potential capacity to sum up all the complexity of the nurturing presence in the figure of the face."[1] The parent's face becomes the center of the universe for the new child, with all of life orbiting around that comforting presence.

Ironically, it is this bond that allows babies to realize they are separate people months later. This early attachment is critical for later self-awareness and connecting to others. As Drs. Henry Cloud and John Townsend wrote, "Attachment is the capacity to relate to God and others, to connect to something outside of ourselves. When we make an attachment, good things are transferred between us and others."[2]

But unlike a human parent who comes and goes, God is our constant face through which we discover our own spiritual faces or true identities. Our longing to know God's love is like the child's for his or her mother, only more significant. As Loder explained, God is "the Face that will not go away."[3]

As parents, we have a continual source of encouragement and focus through relationship with our Father in heaven. The more we focus on who He is, the better we are able to shape that image in our kids. And together, we can take on His features.

To Clone or Not to Clone

Human duplication happens naturally through DNA, but parenting isn't cloning. Strict uniformity is not God's style. We are made in His image, but that likeness includes freedom. He gives us more authentic choices than we could possibly make in our lifetime.

Jon and Tim are not me. They have tried on parts of me, but each of them has his own individual personality or "emotional fingerprint."[4] God's creative genius continues as our kids become who God designed them to be.

Our home had a costume box full of odd disguises: a clown wig, plastic gladiator armor, cowboy chaps, a firefighter's hat, a doctor's stethoscope, anything that would allow our kids to experiment with different characters. (We later succumbed to adding a holster with guns because our sons were devising weapons from anything vaguely gun shaped, such as bananas or partially chewed toast.) Kids need the space to experiment with various roles, like rummaging through that box of costumes: being brave, fighting for good, rescuing from danger, entertaining others by being the star.

As our children grow, we can encourage the possibilities that are uniquely theirs. They will soon learn that their life's course is not simply automatic, but a series of choices. Some are just a matter of preference: liking jazz over rock, surfing over football, blue over red, or architect over engineer.

But other choices are moral and reflect God's character—to show compassion, to forgive, to sacrifice, to share in someone's joy—or not. Hopefully, all the smaller lessons along the way will help our children to find "the way they should go" (Prov. 22:6). /// **GOOD DECISIONS HAVE A FIGHTING CHANCE WHEN A PARENT CHOOSES TO REFLECT GOD'S LOVING NATURE, OVER AND OVER.** /// In the end, children must make that choice for themselves. Parents can't hold God's will to their children's heads like a weapon any more than God did in Eden. Good imitation is a powerful, even likely, possibility, but not 100 percent guaranteed.

Not the Only Pretty Face in the Crowd

Parents have some competition. The harsh reality is that we aren't the only possible models for our young imitators. Cartoon characters, older siblings, friends, grandparents, and famous media stars can leave lasting impressions. The child begins by adopting the beliefs, values, and actions of a favored person, who shapes the child's identity. The child must always wear a red cape, or a blue princess dress, or copy the hairstyle and swagger of an admired person. This esteemed hero or heroine can capture a child's heart because of some rewarding quality, such as bravery, kindness, or acceptance. It can even be an imaginary friend. Tim was especially enamored by cowboys and wanted to wear his prized leather boots to bed. Usually this is a safe game that allows children to practice new roles in a make-believe world.

Children are more likely to imitate people who are warm, nurturing, and trustworthy. They are keen to detect insincere or unreliable folks and will resist their leadership. If we want a following, we can begin by showing our kids genuine affection and attention to their needs. Studies have even shown that children will copy actions that are ridiculous if a trusted person does them first, such as commanding dogs to stop barking.[5]

Imitation is our social glue. It helps us bond to others as we copy their lives. As we empathize with our kids, they learn to relate well to others. Even our emotions are contagious! We want to fit in.

But this also means that lonely children are more vulnerable to negative examples because they want to belong. If children feel ignored or unaccepted by parents, they will look elsewhere. The implications for this in the teen years are enormous, when the storms of peer pressure hit full force. Parents need to get a running start on establishing close connections with their children. We want to be those affirming role models our children can trust, realizing our potential to influence before it's too late.

Here is our greatest incentive: if we enter our children's world, they are more likely to buy into ours. This was demonstrated in an intriguing social experiment with restaurant waitstaff. One group of servers was coached to mimic the remarks of patrons, while another control group did not. The results? Those who repeated customers' words back to them were rewarded with bigger tips.[6]

We imitate those who imitate us. If we reverse the imitation and follow our kids into their world, they just might return the favor. /// AS WE LEARN FROM OUR KIDS, THEY WILL BE MORE EAGER TO LEARN FROM US. ///

Shaping our kids through personal example does have a disclaimer: individual results may vary. As you grow more aware of your own large footprints around the house, you may feel overly confident that smaller feet are following close behind. We know well-adjusted, impactful, and caring individuals who were raised in painful circumstances by broken adults who were anything but good examples. We have also known children who continue to stumble as adults who seemingly had ideal fathers and mothers. Go figure.

Still, using the power of your example is one of the most effective ways to shape your child. No child comes with a guarantee. But at the very least, you have the reward of time spent together, facing the same direction, growing close. Isn't that the greatest outcome of all?

Questions

Have you noticed any of your mannerisms in your child? Which ones?

What do you hope your child inherits from your character?

What traits do you hope your child does *not* adopt?

How are you challenged to change because of your child's imitation?

Part Two

A PLACE TO GROW

We moved eight times before our kids were in high school, but we always found a sturdy tree in every backyard. It was almost a sign that we should live there. Each tree became a unique scaffold on which we could build a fort. Above the ground, below the tallest limbs, we constructed a place where anything could be imagined. It was an unconventional residence for our kids.

We always built the forts together, and their designs were quite simple: at least one floor with open slat walls to look out on the world. Getting up there was part of the adventure.

Our sons' tree house activities changed as they grew. From bravely fighting battles to relaxing in the shade to read a good book, they continued to make each fort a home.

This is what we wanted our family to be: a cooperative, sturdy place to dream and nurture those dreams, where kids and adults felt comfortable and we could all grow up together.

Chapter 6

CREATIVE SPACE
A Garden of Choice

BY JAN

If you look the right way, you can see that the whole world is a garden.
—Frances Hodgson Burnett, *The Secret Garden*

The Physical Space: An Environment for Discovery and Choice

Three small words describe all God's creation, from expanding galaxies to invisible microbes: "It was good." Then when God designed the ideal space for the first humans, He planted a garden. It was also good. So God gave them freedom to eat from every tree on the landscape, except one. There was a single tree, not many trees, that was forbidden. The garden experience was a widely varied, life-tasting feast of beauty, fragrance, flavors, sounds, and textures. Gardens are for growing.

This defines God's parenting style: provide an open creative place that allows the child to grow. *Discovery* and *choice* are essential to God's kid-friendly garden because each object a child inspects is both a choice and a moment of insight. This sense of wonder and curiosity is never meant to be lost.

Our babies evidence this eagerness by shoving each new object into open mouths, as if to say, "I want to know all I can about this world, engaging every single sense!" The more they see, touch, and taste, the more they learn. So as parents, we can encourage that enthusiastic curiosity. Of course, grown adults who still mouth objects would be strange and unhealthy, so how do we help our kids discriminate between dirt and doughnuts without killing their insatiable appetites to learn?

We parents are the child's interpreters of this world. Is it safe? Not always. But we have the Maker who makes it safe. Just as God walked the garden with the first couple, we can hold His hand and our child's in the other until the child's grasp is fully transferred to God. The Master Guide then takes our child to adventures beyond what we, as parents, could dream. The Creator allows us—and our children—to be the bravest explorers of all, the most creative and courageous people on the planet.

We can take our cues from our heavenly Father, who can't wait to show us a hidden waterfall or painted sky, or let us taste an exotic fruit or name a bizarre marine creature. He grants this intoxicating freedom to roam an enormous garden. So we can risk letting our children run through the whole yard. Our God offers both safety and discovery.

What could that look like in an average household well outside of Eden? Our children's garden space included a closet of odds and ends. There were the usual craft essentials of construction paper, glue, and scissors. But there were also some surprises to challenge the imagination: empty spools, random-sized boxes, pieces of cloth with various textures, buttons, pipe cleaners, and seeds. And all of this could be anything one wished.

I set up play areas around each room that rotated throughout the week. Having several good options at a time gave our kids the power to choose as well as discover and create something original. There might be a table with paint, scissors, glue, and paper; a music central with kids' records and a player, along with kid-sized instruments; a building place with blocks, wood scraps, and Legos; or a make-believe area with mini-figures, costumes, and various props.

The lower kitchen cupboards were always fair game to create a percussive orchestra of various tones. Every day, pans, bowls, and Tupperware were spread on the floor, beaten by a variety of kitchen tools. They played this makeshift drum kit for hours making up songs. I just had to watch where I stepped.

My parents confined toys to my bedroom. The rest of the house was for the adults, so play was compartmentalized, separate from their world. I was spared the hovering intervention of adults into my imaginary world, and they were spared the mess. But the big downside was that I have no memories of playing with my mom or dad.

We wanted to draw a different blueprint. We didn't segregate our home into adult versus child. We wanted everyone to feel comfortable in all the rooms. Having hand-me-down furnishings helped: Couch cushions made forts, and we allowed tricycles to be ridden in certain areas. We installed a swing in their bedroom plus a slide for cold winters.

One well-meaning friend argued with my approach, saying, "What will your kids do in someone else's nice house?" But we never had issues with our sons disrespecting another's space. I suspect it was because they had one place they could run free and knew the difference. Our house reflected our values, preferring casual and fun over tidy. Maybe someday we would present a decorator's impeccable interior, but not while raising kids. (And, I will add, not with grandkids either!)

We wanted to send the message that God's world is a big *yes*. This was our version of a widely varied garden. Our small home became an ever-changing frontier populated with cowboys and zoos, young artists and engineers, that daily beckoned and asked, "What will we discover today?"

The variety show continued outside our walls as we expanded our kids' horizons with museums, plays, parades, and hikes. We scoured the local scene for freebies: lawn concerts, exhibits, and historic reenactments. We were regulars at the library.

We wanted to match the good of God's garden by providing quality experiences at a young age. We had a future motive: to increase their appetites for the good in culture. Under the powerful influence of advertising, we can falsely believe that new curiosities are more valuable than the old, in what C. S. Lewis calls "chronological snobbery."[1] But maybe if we provide a steady diet of substantial treats, our kids will choose these over popping faddish gumballs into their hungry minds.

Ultimately, we want adult children who can relate to every sort of person, in any location or season, under every circumstance. This ability to be multicultural in an increasingly complex world doesn't happen without broad exposure. We want to raise Renaissance kids who have an inner quality control. Again, it's learning to distinguish dirt from doughnuts.

An Open Space: Less Is More

I thank You God for this most amazing day: for the leaping greenly spirits of trees and a blue true dream of sky; and for everything which is natural which is infinite which is yes.

—E. E. Cummings

In high school, I had a poster depicting cartoon hippos climbing into a small rowboat with the caption: "Sometimes less is more." In a culture of abundance, that's always a good reminder.

This wise saying was somewhat forced on us by economics. We lived at or below the poverty level in our kids' early years, so of necessity we had less. But that gave us more room in the rowboat. We were inspired to create adventures out of very raw material. This open-ended, make-it-up-as-you-go-along play is now recognized to be essential for developing young minds. Less *is* more.

One blessing of poverty was that we didn't own a TV until Jon was nine and Tim was seven. Even then, it was not our purchase; some friends out of pity gave us their old black-and-white, which we set up in the basement. It needed some kind of weight on a string to hold the dial on a selected channel. Because our kids were older when this set arrived, their creative muscles were trained for more active pursuits.

Our nonacquisition of a TV and its placement at the bottom of our house were deliberate too. We questioned the long-term effects on young eyes and brains focused on flat, brightly lit two-dimensional objects. More concerning was what those children were *not* doing while they sat and stared at the hypnotizing tube.

Now the jury has a verdict: the American Academy of Pediatrics discourages TV viewing in young children—this despite recent US surveys that show preschool children make up the largest TV audience, watching an average of thirty-plus hours a week![2] Again, less is more.

We wanted active, unstructured play, not scripted by either the toy's design or requiring adult supervision. Jane Healy, a leading authority on education, wrote, "A brain which is actively involved and curious is likely to develop stronger connections than one which is merely a passive recipient of learning."[3] So "batteries not included" was always our goal. If a stuffed animal has a programmed voice, our kids won't imagine an original conversation. For us, the more primitive the toy was, the better. Better still, why not create imaginary friends out of clothespins with shoes as their automobiles and feather-pillow mountains rising from a carpet sea?

Something significant is at stake: We want to place the *incentive* inside our kids. We tend to take shortcuts by using enticements that are outside of our children. But if their motivation is solely the carrot on a stick, what happens when there are no more carrots? We deprive our children of developing essential inner qualities when we short-circuit their own passions and drive with shallow, easy rewards.

We want to grow the fire within. Are we helping our children kindle their own interests, or are we always the ones carrying the match and wood? I must continually ask: Is this opportunity going to destroy or enhance my child's ability to choose? How am I enabling that God-given incentive—or am I usurping its power?

Give a toddler a dazzling rainbow-colored gadget, with push-button tunes and automated movement, and the child will end up playing with its box. What every child wants are open-ended choices, not scripted options. It may seem that the kindest work of a parent is to ease this burden of choice, but this cripples the child for real life that demands muscular decisions in adulthood.

We wanted our values to determine our Toyland. Beyond safety and age guidelines, we looked for quality items that could transition into older use. The most used toy in our home was a set of plain wooden blocks. We also liked toys that were aesthetically pleasing, not gaudy, ones that encouraged role-playing or problem solving without obvious choices for a predetermined outcome. Walk down any toy aisle and you quickly realize how quality play for kids does not come easy—or cheap.

That is why less is more when establishing a creative home. If we are engulfed in sound bites and engaging visuals, we can grow deaf to the subtle whispers of honest, raw creative moments. The children who are overstimulated by battery noise and flashy images may struggle to appreciate the quieter joys of digging in the sand or singing to themselves in the silence.

What drives me to fill every space with activity and sounds? Why do I complicate my life with the clutter of consumerism? When was the last time I flew a kite, or turned off the TV and made up a story, or built a cardboard-box fort with my child? Young minds need room to breathe, places to hear their own imaginative voices. /// **I CAN LEAD MY CHILD DOWN THE PATH OF INSPIRATION RATHER THAN THE PATH OF LEAST RESISTANCE.** ///

Think of the smell of creativity rising from a fresh big box of crayons. With all colors untouched, each crayon is equally inviting, from magenta to silver to lime. The newly opened box gives us permission to try a different hue rather than reach for the predictable primaries.

That is how our children view life, without boundaries or boredom, driven to experiment at every turn. Everything is mysterious. We want to applaud that fresh perspective, even within our own souls, for the creative to flourish.

I can function as a brake or accelerator in my child's life. In my cautious moments, I'm tempted to overly censor this discovery, to simplify my child's life (and mine) by removing some crayons, allowing only *my* favorite colors. After all, a parent *is* the child's primary protector. But we can also be the enthusiastic pushers of learning and wonder.

I've taught art classes to children. I start by explaining some new concept, such as perspective, the color wheel, or shape. Then I pass out scratch paper to practice "the rules." This builds confidence for what happens next.

The most challenging moment for children is after the "good" sheets of paper arrive and they each face one large white possibility. As they stare at the blankness before them, you can almost hear their creative wheels hum as they mentally draw their pictures. Some children wait a painful five or ten minutes to pick up brush or pencil, but I never rush the process because this is the most critical moment in the entire art experience, digging deep to exercise their imaginations. Creativity is problem solving, and a bare canvas demands resolution.

But this is also the most challenging moment for those parents who stayed behind to watch. The emptiness of that perfectly clean paper often becomes unbearable after several minutes with no activity. A few well-meaning parents will suddenly pull up a chair and offer suggestions for the picture. Or if a child chooses a brave orange for the sky, some parents jump in with the fact that skies are *not* that color. Others second-guess what the child began to draw: "Is that the right shape for a tree?" Of course, this silences the child's own creative voice.

It's not easy to sit idly, keeping hands and opinions to ourselves as we watch our kids struggle to solve problems in their time and in their way. But this is the necessary discomfort of learning. /// CREATIVITY INVOLVES PAINSTAKING TRIAL AND ERROR. WE DON'T WANT TO DENY OUR KIDS THIS PRIVILEGE. ///

Art, adult-style, is to show off the perfectly white canvas. There are no mistakes, but is there any art? Because when we make that first stroke or mark, we risk ruining the surface. But isn't the purpose of the canvas to paint something? We want to challenge our kids to solve problems, not eliminate them.

Of course this means mistakes will happen—often. So here is one favorite slogan: mistakes allowed. We all learn the most from them. So why try to remove this effective tool?

I'm not a fan of coloring books either, because I know the standard of excellence: color inside the lines. It's true they can develop eye-hand coordination. But ultimately, the heavy black lines discourage true expression and miss the essential life skill of *improvisation*. Our real life requires thinking on our feet, like a skilled jazz musician, to envision what could be, not just playing the obvious notes. If we loosen up, we can allow our children to freely color outside the lines, even outside the book, with any crayon they choose.

Unstructured play also fosters *imagination*. That's why childhood is often called the wonder years. It's a sad day when the small voices, tirelessly asking questions, are quiet. Where did the wonder go?

An open environment leaves room for wonder and doesn't try to fill in the blanks. Wonder is the gift that grows a robust imagination. And imagination is what can change the world.

A Defined Space: Cultivating Specific Gifts

We made our first trip to Disneyland when Jon was almost three. After a long day, we lined up on the crowded curb to watch the closing parade. Tim was secured in his umbrella stroller, but Jon stood tiptoe to see the waving characters and animated floats. Finally, a marching band strode by, with row upon row of gleaming brass instruments and bass drums with Mickey Mouse painted in the center. As we finished cheering for the last song, we reached for Jon's hand but he was not there! Had someone grabbed him, or had he lost sight of us in the excitement and wandered off?

Instinctively, we followed the moving banner that separated us from the parading band. There, next to the drum section, was tiny Jon, caught up in the moment, forgetting his family in the magic of music. Our young leave large clues about their passions and future aspirations, and we must follow.

Parents are like anthropologists living with an aboriginal tribe to learn their culture and unearth their buried relics. We do not create their unique natural gifts, but we can help our kids discover and polish these talents.

Before they could walk, our sons pulled themselves up next to the stereo console and bounced, anticipating songs. One of Jon's very first words was "mooney" for music, demanding another record. Later they constructed "music machines" and made up tunes with words. When Jon was barely five, he volunteered to sing "Away in a Manger" in front of our church, and Tim auditioned and landed a leading role in *Sneetches on Beaches* in school. They were dropping hints, and we began to catch them.

This is why it's important to expose our children to a variety of interests: You never know what will stick. Then when we, as parents, notice a pattern, we can gently encourage those passions. What activity does my child return to again and again? Why is this pastime so enjoyable? How can I deepen this interest without narrowing the choices or quenching my child's own motivation? Is there a related activity that might expand my child's interests?

Our son Tim loved to role-play and would dress in different costumes, as our quick-change artist. So we encouraged this fun by filling a costume chest, but we also took him to see children's plays. This related adventure allowed him to experience both actors and costumes in the context of a story. Tim was later inspired to write several original plays. He became a gifted writer—and he is still comfortable onstage.

We took mental notes of our kids' preferences and kept a casual journal of their milestones. Are they unusually social, do they love words and stories, are they drawn to biology, or are they gifted mechanically or athletically? Over time, we can see the dots connecting and the unique trajectories of their lives. This also allows our kids to tell us who they truly are, as opposed to who we might want them to be. We are merely discovering what is already there, responding to creative impulses that were instilled by God Himself.

Nurture versus Nature

We have God's creative DNA. This goes beyond any parent's ability to play the banjo or sing on key or draw cartoons. All God's children are creative; it is our *nature*. But not all are encouraged in its expression. Nurture follows nature, but both are needed.

Mark and I are often asked if we're musical. When we explain that we play instruments, the response is often, "So that's where your kids got it!" The assumption is that musical skill is simply passed on by genetics. But putting too much weight on *nature* may cause us to neglect the greater role that *nurture* plays in developing specific gifts.

Helping our children dig deeper does not mean we take the shovels out of their hands. It simply means that we find new opportunities for them to explore in areas of interest and cheer them on.

Real encouragement isn't a qualitative judgment about the child personally. Rather than "You are such a good artist," we can comment, "I like the colors you chose and the way you drew that plant," or, "You've really practiced and now you play that piece beautifully!"

On the other hand, criticism should be saved for adult professionals. Similar to pruning only a mature tree, it should never be wielded on sensitive budding talent.

Digging deeper also requires discipline. Our son Jon likened songwriting to an archaeological dig: long hours of combing through soil in the hot sun to find a real treasure. True genius never lies waiting on the surface. Disciplined passion will keep digging.

A wise preschool teacher told me that parents often make the mistake of specializing too early because they are eager to reinforce the child's emerging talent. She added this word of caution: depth follows breadth. This was wise advice.

Because every interest informs another; playing soccer enhances coordination, which conveys rhythm to music lessons that improve math, which encourages logic and a passion for philosophy. That is the genius of holistic learning: it dumps everything on the table and lets the child see all the options. We don't learn in a vacuum, so unnaturally isolating one gift from other streams can developmentally warp our children. Child film stars are the obvious poster kids for this too-early pressure.

Also, who knows if that specialty is just for a season? We can use that current passion to connect our kids to other interests down the road. If they love to read, we can find books about faraway places, or a scientific bent can connect to the world of bugs, and ballet could encourage them to design costumes or listen to opera. Why limit the crayons in the box so soon?

Musical Space: A Whole Brain Stimulant

We believe music is an essential language for kids to learn, not a superfluous luxury reserved for a talented few. Music expresses what cannot be said in any other way. Can we fully describe romance, an unexpected loss, a painful relationship, giddy joy, or even God without music? Music is universal.

We introduced our kids to music for pure enjoyment, but we've since learned that music also has a profoundly positive impact on developing brains. A recent study at the University of Münster in Germany shows that practicing the piano in early childhood expands the mind, literally enlarging it anatomically.[4] This is consistent with Daniel Levitin's writing in *This Is Your Brain on Music*: "Studies of violin players … have shown that the region of the brain responsible for moving the left hand—the hand that requires the most precision in violin playing—increases in size as a result of practice."[5]

Another study of preschool children reported that those who were given six months of piano lessons had much better spatial-temporal reasoning as well as math scores than children who were not.[6] Additionally, the College Board (SAT) finds a 10 percent increase of scores in both verbal and math among students who study music for at least four years.[7]

One educational expert, Howard Gardner, explained that music demands both left-brain and right-brain coordination, including rhythm, expressiveness, following patterns, and culminating in fine motor skills.[8] In other words, music gives the child's whole brain a multitasking workout. Music is not only good for the soul but also good for the mind—especially a child's.

Music lessons are also a great way to blend passion with persistence. Our sons wanted to learn piano quite young, so their practice time needed to be age appropriate. Chubby five-year-old hands were connected to a squirmy body, and we wanted to keep the endeavor positive.

But when older, we held a set time each day of at least thirty minutes, five days a week, for practice. There were numerous protests along the way! Yet because they had chosen their instruments and had agreed to finish the course, we could remind them of *their* commitment.

They also experimented with trumpet, saxophone, guitar, and bass. Practice time could be flexibly moved in the day, but it was nonnegotiable. Eventually, the old adage "You will thank me later for this!" proved true.

Tim recently shared that long hours of practice were ultimately useful as a life skill. Mastering a difficult piece gave him courage and stamina to press through other difficult experiences in life, including in his musical career. As parents, we also need courage to press through any momentary resistance to the greater good. If we take the long view, our children will benefit from that vision and maybe say thanks!

Recently, two sailors participating in an around-the-world race were rescued about two hundred miles off the coast of San Francisco. In the early morning hours, in high seas, their yacht was hit by a massive wave that knocked off the boat's steering mounting. Fortunately, they had spent weeks in physical training in preparation for this race. Immediately, they knew what to do: find the radio, which they had sealed in a waterproof bag. After their miraculous rescue, the captain attributed the hours of practice and training to saving their lives.[9]

The rewards of disciplined focus in any area go beyond simply being good at something. Our children's practices may not save them from near-death experiences, but discipline might be lifesaving in another sense by giving them the inner strength to press through difficult situations. Character is shaped one deliberate step at a time.

Emotional Space: A Climate of Acceptance

Fearing people is a dangerous trap.

—Proverbs 29:25 NLT

Acceptance is the oxygen for sustaining creative life, especially in kids. We open up to the possibilities and can be honest. Worrying about what others think steals our passion. Where there is room for failure, there is room for original thought. Perfectionism kills the creative impulse with the obsession to get it right. We all need to be bad at something before we can be good at it.

We can't expect our kids to turn out just like us, but somehow we half believe this myth. We can be fearful when they have their own nuances and radically different preferences. We often hear "I was nothing like that as a child" from a concerned parent. Of course you were different. Each of us leaves a distinct fingerprint.

The night Tim was born, we discovered our friends were already at the hospital to deliver their baby. It was a small mountain medical center with one labor room, so we were on each side of a curtain, racing to the finish line. I won.

This was our early introduction into the not-so-friendly world of competition between parents and their offspring. If my friend's child wins an award, makes the team, or is progressing faster in some skill, do I succumb to the pressure by pushing my child harder? It's hard not to notice the accomplishments, especially when parents advertise with bumper stickers and newspaper articles.

Mark and I never wanted our kids to feel the pressure of comparison. That is a poison that can discourage their brave efforts as well as steal our joy and destroy our relationship. Mentioning another kid's achievements is also the wrong way to motivate our own. We don't want them to be like anyone else, just themselves. That is a message we can't say enough.

The honest truth is that we, as parents, can feel threatened about the perceived success of other families' kids. I remember having a conversation on the beach with a proud mom whose talented sons had been surfing since they were five. Mine had just learned that summer at a YMCA class at ten and twelve. Had I missed something?

Our insecurity as parents can also lead to an unhealthy glut of choices in our attempt to provide the complete childhood. The garden experience doesn't mean we are continually asking our children what they want. We hope to please them and not deny any good, but making them the center of our universe will confuse them about our role as parent—and maybe shape tyrants.

Taking risks together also models acceptance because whenever we tackle something new, we could fall flat. So we continually challenged ourselves as a family to move beyond what we already knew. We sampled unusual foods, like chorizo and star fruit, bought used ice skates, studied and collected rocks, were certified in scuba diving, and Mark tried both skydiving and cliff paragliding with Tim—once!

Jon was a Cub Scout during the Pinewood Derby years. His first vehicle, he proudly announced, would be a superfast skateboard. He even showed us a diagram he'd drawn on a three-by-five paper. He went on to say he thought it could win Best of Show for originality as well as fastest time.

We knew most kids were sculpting racers with the secret help of dads. These were miniature replicas of actual sports cars, with intricate markings and professional finish. But we kept our anxieties to ourselves.

As grace would have it, Jon's skate won the fastest time. And in that sea of wooden automobiles, it was a standout. It also won Best of Show. We framed Jon's diagram as a reminder.

Baseball was another story. Jon could connect with any pitch in the backyard but for some reason regularly struck out in games. After a few seasons of sitting on the bench, he was ready to move on—and so were we.

Mark's mom, Doreen, would often say to our kids, "You're a winner in my book." We joked that this was the worst encouragement ever. But I get it: simply trying does make everyone a winner of sorts. Acceptance gives kids permission to win by trying.

Finding a Balance between Freedom and Limits

Piano lessons are often equated with rigid words and phrases such as "practice," "metronome," "theory," and "sit up straight." Our kids were anything but rigid, so we struggled to find the right teacher. They especially disliked playing what other composers had written: "Why should I learn this? Someone already wrote it!" And they made little modifications to the scores of Mozart and Beethoven.

Finally, we found Mr. Davis, a piano instructor who appreciated their desire for originality. This wise teacher channeled their creative ambition onto blank composition sheets. They could then memorize both the required pieces of others and learn their own. Mr. Davis also taught them how to improvise without any sheet music at all.

This pianist accepted our kids for who they were and didn't try to give them his musical haircut.

As a parent, I want to strike this same balance between enforcing the rules and encouraging original thought. /// **KIDS NEED BOTH DISCIPLINE AND RESOURCEFULNESS TO NAVIGATE THE UNEXPECTED.** /// Our acceptance of who they uniquely are allows them to find both.

This is similar to my art class, where we began by explaining the "rules." The structure gave the students handles from which to create their own art; otherwise, the assignment would have been too overwhelming. But in the end, each child's composition was one-of-a-kind.

This seems to me a main objective in parenting, to empower my child with both the awareness of the lines and the confident freedom to explore outside them, if necessary. Life is challenging. Believing the best in our kids gives them confidence to color inside as well as outside the lines. Someday they may even draw their own.

Spiritual Space: Recognizing God's Creative Genius

The Master Sculptor of heaven and earth has made us in His image. When we encourage our children to become young creators, they discover the authentic face of God. Even as we carry God's rational and moral image into culture, we also bring a deposit of God's brilliant creativity. He *is* the Creator!

Creativity is essential to the God we want our kids to know and love. Yet we often overlook this aspect or leave this gift on the childhood shelf to gather dust. Our common excuse might be that we, as parents, are not creative. Consequently, we lower the bar and expect little from our children.

This brings us back to Eden, God's good garden. We can reopen our souls to the infinite possibilities of seeing what is good. With our children, we can move beyond our tiny plots of familiar earth, fearfully sown, to take in the whole global landscape. We can imitate the Maker's design to plant in our own homes places for kids to flourish creatively.

Every well-tended garden has a fence. The challenge for parents is to strike the balance between adventurous risk taking while encouraging surrender to the will of God. These are not mutually exclusive. In fact, radical discipleship is a lifetime adventure. Faith is always stepping beyond the known into God only knows what.

Too often, parents can misinterpret the moral will of God as a small, confined space of limited choices. Keeping a long list of "shall nots" leaves a negative impression on sensitive kids. Actually, God's moral lines guarantee lasting freedom in all areas. But our own interpretation can be quite narrow, leaving only a small garden space with an intimidating high wall.

A young person can also misread God's will as too restrictive and rebel against the false belief that creativity thrives only outside of God's lines. Isn't this the age-old problem, going back to the very first garden? This extreme view aborts God's creative genius in our young as they wander alone in a cultural wilderness.

Our kids need two strengths to be effectively creative: the permission to color outside the lines of convention and the humility to remain within the lines of God's good will. Earlier civilizations wisely recognized that creative genius came from outside the person, calling it a "muse." Now we know the Source of creative life. Only as we depend on Him can we be truly inspired.

Our children are composed of dirt and deity, works of clay who hold the Creator's beauty. The study of science or musical scales or drawing in perspective is really to better understand and cooperate with God's ingenious order. We all enter His garden with great humility and respect.

Yes, we have a creative privilege. We dare to name animals, hum a new melody, invent cures for disease, and illustrate our imaginations on cave walls or canvas. We are allowed to be original in the truest sense, inventing what has never before existed. However, our creations are like us, made from preexisting stuff. Our most brilliant achievements are still traceable to the Source.

Your creative child is a reflection of God's genius, because "from him and through him and for him are all things" (Rom. 11:36). We are not the origin and center of creation, as Descartes's influence has suggested. Instead, we are cocreators who partner with God. Our children can be both humbled and confident in possessing their gifts. In this place of grateful surrender, we can live in the painting of God's creative purpose.

Questions

Describe the environment in your home. Is it a child-friendly space, adults only, or mixed?

How could you make your child's space more unstructured, with greater freedom of choice?

Does your child have any special interests and strengths?

How can you build on this enthusiasm?

Chapter 7
PIZZA WITH GOD
Spiritual Formation for Kids

BY MARK

Children are the hands by which we take hold of heaven.
—Henry Ward Beecher

"Do you have peace with God?"

Jon and Tim often overheard this big evangelical question. But children hear spiritual jargon in relation to their own experiences.

Jon figured this was a good opener for a conversation about God. So one morning in his public school kindergarten, he tried it out on a new friend. He gave the question a fresh twist: "Do you have pizza with God at your church?"

To which the friend replied, "No."

So Jon confidently announced, "*We* have pizza with God."

Later that evening, the five-year-old friend asked his parents if they could *please* go to Jon's church because of the pizza—with God, no less. Beyond curious, the parents agreed and came. They were looking for pizza *and* God.

We met this young family the next Sunday at church, and they explained Jon's compelling invitation. But afterward, I wondered, was it truly a misunderstanding, or was it a proper paraphrase? Maybe he got it right, that sharing a pizza is really how God wants to relate to us.

I decided I liked Jon's interpretation of the big question better. It explains peace as having a delicious slice of life with the Creator of the universe. What food is more communal than pizza? And it marks a celebration too, because every party needs pizza.

Perhaps Jon blended that question with Jesus's words in Revelation 3:20, about wanting to come in and share a meal with us. At least he understood the meaning: we can be God's friend, eating slices of pepperoni pizza and trading stories with smiles.

Do we have pizza with God? Trying to explain the invisible God to a small person, we begin to realize how much we both need the tangible to reveal the intangible.

Truth That Can Be Touched

Recently, I watched a young dad twirl his infant son in a hotel pool. Why do I often forget how fun God is? That He delights in delighting His kids, no less than this human parent? And perhaps we are merely the imitation of God's joy over being with us.

That is really the essence of explaining God to a child: we are models of Him. My kids can learn about God through me. Scary proposition, however. Does anything terrify me more than being a replica of God Most High? To not only explain who He is but be a human reenactment of how He moves, thinks, and feels? The spiritual formation of our kids begins here, with our own imperfect faith and everyday example.

This is the brilliance behind the Lord's words to parents in Deuteronomy 6. Called the Shema, or "hear," it leaves no coordinate on the globe where God cannot be spotted:

> Hear, O Israel: The LORD our God, the LORD is one. Love the LORD your God with all your heart and with all your soul and with all your strength. These commandments that I give you today are to be on your hearts. Impress them on your children. Talk about them when you sit at home and when you walk along the road, when you lie down and when you get up. Tie them as symbols on your hands and bind them on your foreheads. Write them on the doorframes of your houses and on your gates. (Deut. 6:4–9)

Imbedded in this passage is a winning strategy for explaining God to our kids: It's on-the-job training. We use the show-and-tell of everyday moments to transmit spiritual life.

Jon and Tim first heard my brief conversion story on the way back from the local dump. We had just disposed of the trash and were driving home when the conversation ensued. At that unceremonious moment, they insisted that I lead them in a prayer to receive Christ. Caught off guard, I was reluctant because I wanted Jan to share the experience. Plus, the whole setting seemed too earthy and common. Where was the special music, the angelic voices, or glowing light? The dump? But they insisted, "Now!"

The Shema became our blueprint for communicating God's life.

Although we had nightly prayers and a short Saturday morning devotion, our best conversations happened on the fly as we ate, drove to school, shopped, played catch, and even when we took out the trash.

On long road trips, we played a game with clues to guess objects: "I'm thinking of something blue and white and round …" When we think about God with us at all times, we can find all kinds of clues to describe Him:

- "I wonder how God makes every snowflake different?"
- "Let's ask God to help you find your lost backpack."
- "What a beautiful morning God gave us to visit the lake."
- "Since we can't go to the park because it's raining, maybe God has a better plan."
- "I want to tell you what I read this morning in my Bible and how it helps me today."

We can let our children know, through ordinary moments, that God is relevant and present. It's pizza with God.

We Are All Spiritual

We are spirit people. So all parents shape their children spiritually, whether actively or passively. The atheist, the alcoholic, the religiously abusive—all are nurturers of some sort. There is never a spiritual vacuum. What we believe about ourselves, this world, and life itself determines how we raise our kids.

This awareness, that humans aren't just physical beings, caused Jan and me to see our kids multidimensionally: body, yes, but also soul, mind, emotions, and spirit. We wanted to nourish the whole child.

It's impossible to separate the whole into parts, the spiritual from the mental or physical. Even when we bite into a pizza, it engages our minds and emotions, not just our stomachs. Each part of us influences the others.

Back to the pizza: I like that analogy because it combines knowing God, a spiritual Being, with a favorite food. This is authentic religion—not just ethereal, but a sink-your-teeth-into-it experience (pun intended).

We wanted to erase the lines between the secular and sacred for our kids. Special does not mean separate. Supernatural does not mean unnatural. When we set up for church in the gym, we brought Nerf balls for the kids who came early. During the week, we prayed for parking spaces, skinned elbows, making new friends, difficult teachers, and to find lost toys.

Right after we moved to plant a church in the South, Tim qualified for a travel soccer team. His first game was on a Sunday, so he wanted to wear the new uniform to church. In the Bible Belt, this was close to the buckle. I wondered what splash this would make on the church culture to see the pastor's son arrive ready for the game, cleats and all. But to raise the issue would contradict our belief that God is a part of all of life—especially soccer for an eight-year-old boy. He wore his uniform.

A Child's View

Children are born curious and are wonderstruck by things we find commonplace. They are in awe of the wind that moves the plants, the buzz of a single bee around a bright pink rose, the smell of dirt, and the prickle of grass on their small feet.

Children are naturally open to the supernatural. They are fresh spiritual beings, not yet dulled by adult sensibilities or matter-of-fact answers. They expect to be surprised and amazed. This means we can speak confidently about unseen realities to a child with great freedom. Their trust is second nature because children are born understanding the language of simple faith.

When Jesus said, "Let the little children come to Me," He wasn't trying to appease the proud parents in the crowd. He really wanted to be with those kids. He found a quality within that eager cluster of high voices that He missed in the older followers.

His explanation was remarkable: Unless the staid big people became like those irreverent, noisy, bold children, they would not participate in His Father's plan for this world. It's really up to the kids, those who easily believe and follow with great expectations. This openness gives us a tremendous advantage, as believing parents, to explore God's love with our kids.

Our cabin's outdoor deck was a gigantic playpen for our sons. It was perpetually cluttered with bikes, trucks, and other wheeled toys that wandered outside. One summer afternoon, a rainstorm was threatening to soak that space, so we pointed to the dark clouds and asked Jon to collect his toys and come inside. A few minutes later, we noticed he was still engaged with his trucks, so we reminded him all his toys were about to get wet.

"It's okay, Momma. I asked Jesus to not have it rain right here."

We thought getting wet would be a safe reminder to Jon about listening, so we let him continue to play. But God had a better lesson in mind: that patio stayed dry all afternoon, while the rain swirled around our house. I could almost hear Jesus say again, "Let the little children come to Me."

Our adult minds have learned to quarantine the sacred from the secular, so our spiritual realities may not touch any other parts of our lives, like different foods safely separated on a plate. But for the young child, every person, event, or object floats in a spiritual soup. Children have an innate sense that there is an epic story behind the obvious world. They relish fantasy because they sense there is another reality, so much more than meets the eye. And they are right.

We complicate our believing as we grow old, adding more conditions, clauses, and reasons why we can't completely let go and trust. So in considering how to spiritually form our children, we also need to remember they have a lot to teach us too.

The Challenge

One dreamy Sunday morning, Jon crawled downstairs in his blanket sleepers and climbed into my arms. Setting down my competing coffee mug, I nestled him in one arm as we both stared at my open Bible.

Jon, alert without caffeine, asked me, "What are you studying?"

I replied softly, "I'm reading Genesis 1, and I'm going to teach on 'The Rest of God.'"

Jon asked innocently, "Did you teach on the other part of Him last week?"

Explaining spiritual truths to kids is a challenge only because we think like adults. Children, thankfully, don't learn like grown-ups. To bring our children along, we must follow Christ's example: we leave our world to enter theirs. Just as a missionary learns the language and culture of a faraway people, a parent must cross over into the child's world.

But the challenge for parents is even greater because our children keep shifting their language and culture as they develop. Jon and Tim at two years were not the same at eight or sixteen. We must adapt over and over to communicate well.

Isaiah 40:11 says, "He gently leads those that have young." We can't drive our kids any faster than their short legs can walk. On our spiritual journey, we must travel slowly with children. We walk at their pace, paying attention to their energy and interest level.

Jan and I held a "Jesus Time" every Saturday morning with our kids. Children love routines but are easily bored. So we didn't start with *My Utmost for His Highest*. We put the emphasis on fun. Rather than enduring a long adult monologue, we made each lesson bite-size, creative, and hands-on active. We started with a five-minute illustrated story. Then we might act it out or draw a picture of what we learned. We always sang. We ended with everyone praying about whatever was on the mind.

Our kids always looked forward to this time. We believe it built in them an expectation to hear from God. The consistency modeled the importance of spiritual discipline. It gave them an appetite for God's Word.

Most of all, we always wanted our kids to associate pleasant with knowing God. We wanted to err on the side of creative learning rather than accumulating facts.

We aren't trying to sneak a serious, dull God into the room under the guise of fun and games. This isn't bait-and-switch. That was often my impression of youth group antics, that we were smothering a stuffy subject with lots of frosting and sprinkles, like swallowing our medicine without gagging. But that's because our perception of God is faulty. Truthfully, He is the most appealing Person in the universe.

We painstakingly size our kids with shoes and clothing and give away what is outgrown. What we teach our children about God must also match their age, like clothes that fit. The Bible isn't children's literature. A toddler only needs to know about a big, kind God who loves everyone and keeps us safe. But a teenager must be allowed to wrestle with the problem of evil or the brutality of the crucifixion without having nightmares about the Antichrist. This means that we, as parents, must truly know our very complex children inside and out to realize what truths can be safely digested. It's never a one-size-fits-all answer.

The media we use must also be a good fit. Puppets, plays, and cutouts that help a preschooler learn would insult an adolescent who wants the challenge of an open Bible and honest dialogue around a fire pit. Our kids moved from short stories and sing-along tunes to dissecting T. S. Eliot and uncovering spiritual themes in Wagner. The target keeps moving, and that keeps us on our toes.

Of course, all ages, even seasoned adults, crave stories that illustrate this invisible realm, like a full-color pop-out picture book. /// SPIRITUAL TRUTHS NEED TO BE TOUCHED, HEARD, TASTED, AND SMELLED, USING ALL OUR SENSES TO GRASP THEIR REALITY. /// A great story is like a clothes hanger that displays beautiful but abstract concepts. Without this real-life example, new truths collapse in piles like garments on the floor of the mind.

We have a tendency to compartmentalize our relationships with God so He is partitioned off from what we enjoy or fear or must do. An unintended sad lesson that children learn from formal classrooms is that their education in math, English, or history doesn't always apply to real life. Kids adapt to running on two tracks: what they must memorize as irrelevant facts and what actually benefits and engages them in the real world.

That dualism can easily infect any formal spiritual training as well. A child can parrot a scripture, including chapter and verse, but it might not help them with school cliques or fear of the dark. Eventually, kids can assume the stories of the Bible don't apply to their dreams or daily struggles. But when conversations about God happen informally, under a tree, on the beach, at the game, it shatters that assumption.

Learning from all of life creates a holistic spirituality. God is as natural and necessary as a trip to the dump. As parents, we too can be subconsciously plagued with two-world thinking, which assumes the spiritual realm doesn't intersect the physical. This creates believers only at church, not at work, play, or school. But when spiritual insight happens in ordinary moments, we are naturally supernatural. We realize God impacts all of our lives.

Of course, none of our life lessons for kids will be absorbed without two essentials: play and honesty.

Every Truth Also Has a Feeling

Why did one find it so hard to feel as one was told one ought to feel about God? ... The whole subject was associated with lowered voices; almost as it if were something medical.

—C. S. Lewis, "Sometimes Fairy Stories May Say Best What's to Be Said"

Children live in a whimsical world; they simply can't learn unless they are having fun. It's easy to take ourselves too seriously when we open the door to spiritual themes. We can be unnaturally solemn as we approach the sacred. Maybe we've been conditioned by years in church where we sat up straight and tried *not* to laugh.

We can also fall into a moralistic pit, which mires us in legalism: God will be angry or disappointed or distant if you ... (fill in the blank). This is not fun for kids—or adults. An anxious, sensitive child can become preoccupied with harmful obsessions and miss the whole point: God is love.

Yes, we take God seriously, but never ourselves. Laughter, especially at us, is more compelling than all our self-conscious piety. /// WE CAN COMMUNICATE MORE THEOLOGY THROUGH A FAMILY DANCE PARTY OR TELLING STORIES AROUND A CAMPFIRE THAN SITTING STIFFLY FOR AN HOUR. /// Hilarity in designing a birthday cake for Jesus creates more happy feelings than a lecture on the incarnation.

God is not a construct but a Person who engages all our feelings, positive or negative, depending on our experiences.

It's wonderful to think that Jesus's first miracle was turning plain water into fine wine. This is a great illustration of how God wants to reveal Himself to our kids in unexpected pleasures. We can taste and see that He is good.

Trigonometry left a bad emotional taste in my mouth because of my demanding teacher. Most learning has a subjective flavor. We bring feelings into our facts. Truths about God can have a positive or negative charge, depending on the context.

If a child is worried or upset and someone speaks harshly to him or her, can the child hear the words? Even when quoting some uplifting verse, it can have the reverse effect: "We know that all things work together for good" can feel like a rebuke to a child who only needs an understanding hug.

A wonderful truth expressed in a negative way is like a spiritual mud pie that leaves the person slimed with bad feelings instead of encouraged. As Emerson said, "What you are stands over you the while, and thunders so that I cannot hear what you say to the contrary."[1] Emotions are contagious. Our porous kids quickly absorb our unchecked feelings of blame, irritation, or fear—no matter how heavenly the topic.

We want to carve pathways for our kids to return to God again and again—not dig a moat. Unlike Moses who beat the rock when God was not upset, we want to draw an accurate picture of a welcoming God.

If we hope to communicate heart truth, it must resonate with us first. Innocent kids are professionals in the world of pretend, so they can spot phony platitudes. Do our words come from deep conviction or simply from our mouths? Tim described a teacher who had "a smile on her lips and mean eyes." Kids are disarmingly honest. They respond best to our own authenticity.

The Magic of Narnia

I felt smug after completing grad school. At twenty-five, my mind was fattened with minutia about ancient manuscripts, the latest research on marriage, and how to analyze leadership styles. I came by this honestly as a strictly nonfiction reader. After all, why waste time on what isn't factually supported? Twenty-five was also my age when our first child was born. Then I discovered the deeper wisdom of make-believe. Then came Narnia.

Prior to college, I had not been a believer in God, so I was unfamiliar with C. S. Lewis. Especially after years of education just absorbing textbooks, Lewis's writings were a monumental discovery. I began with *Mere Christianity* and a few of Lewis's essays. But when Jon turned three, I wanted to explore the world of Narnia with my little son.

Though Jon was young, Narnia captured his imagination. Eventually, both Jon and Tim sat on my lap by the hour each night listening to stories of Lucy, Peter, Edmund, and Susan. Jon sat through three readings of the entire set, and Tim lasted two complete series before he switched to Lewis's Space Trilogy.

These nightly readings shaped us in surprising ways. The first indirect benefit was the bond it created. This shared experience drew us together as if we had taken a short, exciting trip. Night after night, the adventures transported us to another world created by Lewis. The word *Narnia* itself is a nostalgic term for all of us: it means togetherness.

Another plus was that Jon and Tim were able to learn about God without ever using the term. Lewis believed that most people, religious or atheists, have their front doors guarded and locked with preset God opinions. Dogma and open thinking don't go hand in hand. But Lewis was the master at creating stories that could sneak past the "watchful dragons."[2] /// **FANTASY ALLOWS THOUGHTS ABOUT GOD TO ENTER THROUGH A SIDE WINDOW.** ///

For me, my emotionless God of the Right Answers came to life through the lion Aslan. His character is Christlike. The imaginative stories of this compassionate yet regal creature ironically made God seem truer. My nonfiction landscape brightened in the light of Lewis's brilliant fiction. Sterile truth was warmed by emotion.

Another wonderful advantage was that Lewis introduced Jon and Tim to the world of intelligent thought. They learned to appreciate the elegance of his well-crafted tales, how he wove the plot and characters into an intriguing and satisfying whole. The Chronicles of Narnia eventually drew Jon and Tim into Lewis's other books, instilling an appetite for other great literature. Whenever Switchfoot's music is described as "thinking rock 'n' roll," we believe Lewis deserves some credit.

The fantastic tales of Narnia fed Jon's and Tim's own imaginations. They sat spellbound picturing the details of every scene on the high-definition screens of their minds. We believe this lengthened their attention spans as they sat for an hour or more each time just listening. This ability to focus, tuning out distractions for long periods of time, is vital for developing spiritual ears as well as musical.

The Narnia stories can easily apply to all kinds of situations. Jill and Eustace remembering the signs, the insolent guilt of Edmund, the bravery of the small mouse Reepicheep—these became the backdrop for many important conversations. The stories inspired curiosity about their own stories, where no subject was off-limits.

Passing the Torch

When the summer Olympics came to the United States in 1996, the lit torch was carried north on Pacific Coast Highway, a few blocks below our house. We ran to join the crowd lining the street to cheer the participants. Right in front of us, a man in a wheelchair handed the torch to a muscular athlete who sprinted away. It was fascinating to realize this flame had been passed all around the globe between thousands of people.

This wasn't a perfunctory exercise where they pretended to pass a flame on an extinguished torch. It was an actual fire that could burn your face or light an oil-filled caldron for millions to see.

Handing off our faith is a lot like that pre-Olympic ceremony. The whole point is to pass it on so everyone can enjoy it, starting with those closest to us. It's not a private candle we take home; it belongs to the whole world.

Passing the torch begins here: We light our own flames and keep them lit. We make sure we have fire we can pass along. We are already running the race of life, so we aren't adding something new. It's about how we run and what we are carrying and who is running behind us with an open hand. Real faith is a lifestyle.

I'm not passing along my convictions like a fluffy worn comforter that simply keeps my kids warm and safe—or saves me trouble later in life. It's a brilliant fire that can play a crucial role in God's master plan to light up the world.

Our children have divine assignments to run their individual races with their own fires. As Jan and I recognized our kids' capacity for spiritual growth, it encouraged us to involve them in our own opportunities to serve. Segregating our spiritual experiences from our kids' is a common but unfortunate barricade. But having our children with us allowed them to see us pray for an injured child, meet a family whose dad lost his job, or hear a heckler make fun of my pastoral message. Each experience gave our kids a hands-on demonstration of God's love that we hoped would place their own callings within reach.

At a conference in Baltimore, our kids rested on chairs next to us, eyes shut, as we listened to the closing speaker. We had no idea that one child was taking in the message that we can all actively participate in following Jesus.

After the teaching, anyone could come onstage to receive prayer or to pray. I glanced down to check on our two sleeping bundles and was startled that one was missing. Where was Jon?

I quickly got up and ran through the huge conference center hallway, racing one way, then the next, shouting his name, and checking every bathroom. After ten breathless minutes, I returned to Jan, saying desperately, "He's gone!"

Then we realized the one place we hadn't looked: the stage. There, one hundred feet in front of us, was our small son with his hands on some man's stomach, praying for him to be healed. He had listened beyond what we could have imagined—certainly more than we had. It was not an issue of age or height, but heart.

We wanted to hand Jon and Tim genuine opportunities, not just tokens. A child can often detect a pretend platform in which we already know the outcome and our goal is manipulation of the child's will. We wanted our kids to make authentic choices for good and take risks to discover their own gifts and the size of God's grace. This could not happen in an incubator in which we controlled the variables.

If I could travel back in time as a parent, I would find more everyday opportunities to make a difference with my kids. It was often easier to deliver the grocery bag to a hungry family or encourage the person who was hospitalized on my own. My do-over would include looking for more pathways that allowed my children to touch lives.

Protecting the Flame

The good news of a child's open heart also means that it can be easily wounded and influenced. Our spiritual house needed a door with a window to discern which people or opportunities were in the best interest of our kids' spiritual health. In other words, we tried to protect them from dysfunction in the church family.

When children are raised in a ministry-oriented home, they can observe a lot of brokenness along with the happy stories of redemption. The most painful details often involve difficult personalities within the family of faith: antagonistic, critical, or plain picky, these toxic conflicts can wear down the hopeful soul, especially a child's.

Parents need to carefully define what being authentic means for their children. We decided to never revisit these skirmishes in front of our kids. The underbelly of any well-intentioned community does exist, but we felt it was too burdensome to lay that occasional reality on our innocent kids. These were not their struggles, and they didn't yet have the depth of field to properly sort through the mess. Without adequate armor to protect their open spirits, they would only be wounded in battles that were never theirs.

This meant we needed to practice good spiritual hygiene, not just for our own souls' survival, but also for our children's. A wise friend once explained, "It isn't how well you pretend but who you actually are that determines what happens next." So we could not ignore the damaged relationships but needed to drive through the mud to a clear place of reconciliation.

When I overheard a church acquaintance criticize me to others, I faced three choices: I could air my grievances to my children on the way home, sweep the hurtful words under a thick rug—or face the uncomfortable situation privately with the person. Because if I live with that bitterness toward the person or the church or even God Himself, what is hidden will eventually infect my kids. My attitudes are contagious, not just my words. And my actions will speak loudest of all.

How do I feel about God? Am I satisfied? Comfortable? Cynical? Disappointed? Indifferent? Am I on fire? That torch in my hand will be passed to my children more substantially than any religious education. If I want my children to grow spiritually, I must stay alive. The parable of the airline oxygen mask comes to mind.

We often wrestled with which schools our kids should attend, or discussed the influence of a teacher or what friendships to encourage. But all of these variables are dwarfed by the power of our influence on our kids. We, as parents, must envision who our children can become in God's story, then be that ourselves.

The balance of living outwardly *and* discipling our children is a great challenge. But who we are is the most important factor regarding changing the world and passing our faith to our kids. Our love for people who need Jesus and our passion for our kids will ultimately leave a deposit of both. Of all the variables at our disposal, who we are, in values lived out loud, is the greatest predictor of who our children will become.

In the end, it's really all about having pizza with God.

Questions

What impact did your childhood home have on your spiritual life?

How is your relationship with God now?

How do you want your child to relate to God?

How can you practice the Shema, of talking to and about God 24-7?

Chapter 8

THANK YOU FOR PASSING THE SALT

The Power of Our Words

BY JAN

---

en·cour·age [en-kur-ij, -kuhr-] verb
1. to inspire with courage, spirit, or confidence.
2. to stimulate by assistance, approval, etc.
3. to promote, advance, or foster.

It was easy to read toddler Jon's mind: *The mud in my grandfather Poppy's rose garden is fresh and begging to be squished with my hands and bare feet.* But before we could pull those chubby appendages away from the temptation, saying, "No, no," my wise grandfather said to him, "Thank you for not playing in the rose garden!" And magically, Jon looked but did not touch.

This was one of our earliest lessons on the power of words to shape our kids' behavior. My grandfather spoke to the potential for cooperation in a two-year-old great-grandson who loved dirt, and Jon rose to the occasion. His desire to meet Poppy's positive expectations won over his muddy curiosity.

We can never overestimate the shaping power of our words. Creation was birthed through God's voice: "Let there be … and it was good." In the same way, our small family universe can be formed by our vocabulary. We can speak into existence a thirsty wasteland or cultivate a nurturing garden.

My grandfather had learned the secret of using language to create good. Words not only describe our present or past performance, but they can also define the future. Even Poppy's table etiquette included a compelling statement of gratitude: "Thank you for passing the salt." How could we not want to comply?

A parent is the child's main source of encouragement. When I researched the word *encourage* online, it was in the top 20 percent of all searches. How desperately we all must need it. *Encourage* comes from two Anglo-French words that mean "to make, or put in," plus "courage or heart." So that is my strategic assignment as a parent: to strengthen the heart of my child. In fact, looking up the word *encourager* in a thesaurus lists the first main entry as "father/mother." What a telling reference, that I can be that primary voice of courage to my child. I'm not just stating the obvious. I am shaping my child's future.

An older friend of mine often called her daughter the "racehorse." She explained that her tendency was to be poky, the last to the table, slow to finish chores, and rarely on time. Pointing this out to her young daughter seemed only to make her discouraged and even slower. So she began to speak to her daughter's potential for speed. She noticed when she finished on time and congratulated her on any glimmer of acceleration. Only then did my friend see improvements in her daughter's plodding. She rose to meet her mother's *encouraging* words.

The late Anne Ortlund described children as "wet cement."[1] We inadvertently tested this idea on Tim when he was not quite one year old. After I buckled him in his car seat, he reached out his hand and I accidentally slammed it in the rear car door. Even worse, I locked the keys in the car with the engine running. As he screamed in agony, I ran down the slope from our driveway to grab the extra car key from Mark, yelling for help. But adding to this perfect storm, Mark couldn't hear me because he was using a chain saw!

After a full five minutes, we rescued Tim's mangled hand from the slammed door. As we sped to the emergency room, around each mountain curve, we wondered if he would ever have normal use of that hand again. We braced for the doctor's verdict.

"He'll be fine," the doctor said, then smiled.

What? Just look at those tiny mutilated fingers!

"He only has soft cartilage. No hard bones yet. He's good!"

We felt enormous relief to know how malleable our little one was. Yet this also describes how moldable our children are in every area of their lives, especially while young. Accidents happen, but so can encouragement. We can use this tool, our words, to shape them at any age.

We easily use words to point out the glaring mistakes: stop playing with your food, your room is a mess, you forgot your homework again. Our communication can become one cautionary tale after another. Or we can notice what is right, thus empowering our children to make another good choice, again and again.

/// **WHEN WE CATCH OUR KIDS MAKING GOOD CHOICES, THE KEY IS TO COMMENT SPECIFICALLY ON WHAT WE NOTICE.** /// You can put a positive spin on just about anything: "I understand you hate broccoli. I'm glad you have opinions, but you still need to eat it!" "Look how much fun you had playing with your trucks. Now you can put them all away."

Once, when Jon was asked to clean up his toys, he replied, "It's okay. I asked Jesus to pick them up."

I responded, "Look, Jon, God has answered your prayers! You have two hands!"

Overwatering: Global Praise

Our children are seedlings who drink our encouragement like water. Without enough moisture, young plants whither, but an overwhelming deluge can swamp a fragile plant. One gushing verbal fire hose to avoid is global praise. These grandiose words put our children in uncomfortable spotlights, with expectations impossibly large and vague: "That's a good boy." "You are so beautiful, handsome, smart …" "What a sweet girl you are."

These vast "you are" words place a heavy burden on the child, because they focus on the child's whole being, not some controllable action.

This was one of the hazards of being in ministry with children. Church culture can breed moralistic phrases. Well-intentioned folks assumed it was polite to pepper our kids with saintly descriptions and heavenly accolades: "I bet you want to be a pastor just like your daddy!" "You are such a perfect little family." "I just love your kids!" (We heard that one from complete strangers.)

Global praise is like an ethereal floating halo that leaves our children wondering how they can possibly continue to please or what they must do to remain on that pedestal. These overbearing words can also be manipulative, and the child can sense the not-so-subtle twist: "A good girl wouldn't do that...." "Be a little man and wash the car." "You're a brave kid, so stop crying."

This is counterfeit encouragement that uses external praise to control the child's behavior rather than giving the child a clear assessment of his or her own ability to make good choices.

Within our four walls, Mark and I wanted encouragement that was down-to-earth, tangible, and bite-size. Truly encouraging words are laser focused on specific traits and actions: "That was kind of you to share your toy with him." "I like how you organized your crayons." "You have good eyes to notice those spots on the giraffe."

Parents do have an incredible advantage: all children want to please their parents. When we tell them we are pleased, they believe us.

Not All Words Are Created Equal

No one really believes the old children's rhyme about sticks and stones, but we do throw phrases around carelessly, especially when we feel defeated by little humans. Mark and I discovered that all words are not created equal. Some have a longer shelf life, like toxic time-release capsules whose ill effects are not immediately felt.

Two lethal words that we tried to avoid in any contest were "always" and "never": "You *never* listen." "You *always* forget to make your bed." "You will *never* like that food." "I *always* have to clean up after you."

"Always" and "never" are nails that seal up young hearts with ugly contents inside. We may feel vindicated in our frustration, but the finish line for any desired outcome just got substantially moved. Plus, these words are simply not true. They are exaggerations, at best, and unfair pronouncements that *dis*courage rather than encourage the child to change. It's hard to argue against always and never when you are small.

There were two other words, however, that had the opposite effect. These words became our best friends: "I'm sorry." Of course we lost our tempers along with our minds some days, using "always," "never," and other regrettable words. We could see the damage in our children's eyes and realized we had crossed every line of sane authority. In our attempt to control behavior, we had misbehaved, badly. We knew it. Our kids knew it.

/// WHY ARE THESE TWO WORDS, "I'M SORRY," SO DIFFICULT FOR PARENTS TO SAY? /// Is it because we justify our overreacting based on our children's bad behavior? Or do we believe it will lessen their respect for us? And we will have less control if we admit our faults?

Actually, these are the most powerful two words in any parent's vocabulary. They not only heal relationships but also model humility, the jewel of maturity. Only when we admit our failures can we come to an honest understanding of the situation: "With humility comes wisdom" (Prov. 11:2).

One sunny day, Mark decided to repaint our cabin's front porch, so of course four-year-old Jon wanted to help. Armed with a small brush, Jon was instructed to paint white only the vertical posts on the rail. But when Mark turned around, Jon was also applying white paint to the brown house.

Mark flew into action, abruptly grabbing Jon's brush and scolding him. "I told you, paint only the posts! Look at the extra work you made for me!"

Jon was crushed, as large tears betrayed his unnaturally brave face. Mark wanted only to efficiently paint our porch. Instead, our son had been inadvertently coated—with shame. It seemed practical to finish the project while the brushes were wet. But it was more pressing to heal the wound while it was fresh. So Mark stopped and put down his brush, and through paint-smeared hugs, they were able to talk through where each had been wrong.

This episode not only got the deck painted, but also Jon learned that he could make mistakes, be honest, and move on. His daddy had said he was sorry for his angry response; Jon could also admit he hadn't listened very well. Their parent-child bond was strengthened in that transparent exchange. And Jon happily helped with many more projects.

The villains in the gospel stories are the Pharisees, those always-right religious people we disdain. Extreme fundamentalists. Right on truth, wrong on love. They majored in the minors and minored in the majors. And when you're always right, it's hard to ever admit that you're wrong.

But if there's anything that needs modeling in the spiritual home, it is that very thing, to be transparent about our flaws. There's a lot of truth, not just love, wrapped up in those two little words "I'm sorry." We are all humans who make mistakes. So why are we more comfortable with being right and so awkward with apologies?

Saying "I'm sorry" admits that people are important. And even if we, the parents, are absolutely, blindingly right, how we handled the situation might have been wrong. Fortunately (or unfortunately), Mark and I had numerous opportunities to practice the short phrase "I'm sorry." While raising kids we said it often to each other, day after day. We still do.

Margins matter. Sometimes conversations in our home had more to do with our lack of sleep or how tightly we'd packed our schedule that week. Our best intentions unravel when our bodies are pushed too hard.

I vividly remember a late afternoon when I came home exhausted and had no patience for my son not cleaning his room. I snapped and began to yell uncontrollably that *he would get in there and get it done*! Then in horror, I realized he was cowering under the kitchen table, terrified by my tone. But my tone was just an extension of my already-frayed emotions that had surfaced like pent-up magma exploding from a volcano—but over a messy room? I broke down crying and hugged my frightened son, apologizing for my ridiculous overreaction. My angry outburst really had it origins in my overstuffed calendar, and my child was just an innocent bystander.

Encouraging words need room to incubate. They flourish in open space but get squeezed out by hurry. When time is precious, we keep our sentences clipped and cut out words we believe are extraneous, such as "I love you" or "Please" or "How are you today?" We insert hurry words, which are often tense and utilitarian: "Come on!" "Not now!" "Stop that!"

When encouraging words are scarce, we sometimes need to look no further than our bloated schedules. Encouragement needs a favorable climate to grow in our homes.

Listening: The Other Half of the Conversation

When our toddlers were learning first words, we both worked hard at mutual understanding. We were quick to interpret "bah" for ball and "num-num" for hunger. They were learning to speak, but we were also learning a skill: to listen. The struggle to truly hear our children, even beyond their precise words, never ends. We can never stop asking, "What are you *really* trying to say?"

Listening is a parent's lifeline to the child. Our communication must be reciprocal for our relationship to thrive. Most of us are not born good listeners and can even become hearing impaired after regular assaults of children's chatter. If we were honest, we'd often rather hear our own voices than wade through dialogue with a small person.

The long-range impact of truly hearing our kids is that it teaches them to be good listeners. Not only is this a huge benefit for us parents, who want our young to hang on our every word; it's also an enormous advantage for our children in navigating future relationships. Good listeners make good friends.

To improve our listening abilities, Mark and I learned several kid-friendly communication skills. First, we discovered that children listen with their eyes, so we must return the favor. We didn't want to fit the caricature of a parent who mumbles behind the newspaper. Of course, there are moments when looking at our kids is impractical, such as driving in heavy traffic, but whenever possible we tried to make eye contact on their level. This was also how we could be sure they heard us!

We also practiced reflective listening, simply trying to repeat what we heard using different words. This may seem redundant or obvious at first. But it has two wonderful rewards: the listener must pay attention, and the speaker knows you want to understand.

It's insightful how often we get the message wrong. We already know what we want to hear, so it's easy to pin our ideas onto our children's words, or let our fears finish the sentence, or rush to fix the problem: "I hate my teacher." "I got kicked at recess." "I'm afraid of the dark."

Listening is like stepping onto a thinly iced pond: we carefully test our weight with each step. Our involuntary response is to unleash our own loud voice, but if we do, the conversation will plunge into frigid waters. The main goal is to keep them talking. These conversations become increasingly needed as our children age and drop more seismic verbal bombs: "I want to quit college." "I just met my future husband." "I'm not sure I believe in God."

When a child throws down an explosive topic—at any age—the parent's best option is to dig underneath the words to the heart of the matter. Try to identify with the child's feelings first: "You must be feeling sad at school." "You were embarrassed by that kid's words?" "It must feel lonely."

Children, like all of us, want to be understood. If they sense you are trying to relate to their world, they will invite you in further.

When we truly listen, we want to know more, so insightful questions will naturally follow. Again, the goal is to understand the person—not to correct—so keeping an open ear and heart is essential but not always easy.

"You don't want to go to school today. Tell me what you like or don't like about your new class."

"You want to move to Australia. What appeals to you about the country?"

"You want to dye your hair blue. What shade were you thinking?"

This is not an interrogation. Instead, we are detectives looking for clues in body language, tone, and emotions. What is this person really saying behind the words? All of us, including children, do not always *mean* what we say!

Mealtimes provide an excellent playing field for back-and-forth conversation. We can practice our table manners by giving each speaker time to finish his or her thoughts: "Let's allow him to tell his whole story." We can prime the pump by asking what were the best and worst parts of the day. It is often hardest for us, as parents, not to interrupt.

Good listening opens our children's souls to share their deepest thoughts. But when we voice our opinions too quickly, we can shut that door of vulnerability. Jesus advised, "Don't throw your pearls to pigs," referring to folks who won't appreciate your words. Kids are quick to discern the pigs from pearl enthusiasts—those who will treasure their insights. As we polish each pearl, we are rewarded with greater openness. This exchange, in the safe house of listening, will build an authentic bond that can last a lifetime.

Criticism: The Dark Side of Speech

All children absorb information about themselves from the important people around them. When very young, they are especially sensitive to adult opinions. These powerful words form children's views of themselves, just as those in authority also describe other facts, such as the world is round, lemons are sour, and the stove is hot. Children believe what we tell them.

These adult opinions can either become buried gemstones or act like undetonated mines in the fertile soil of the child's personality. Each child will one day unearth and act on what lies inside.

As natives of the sophisticated first world, surviving the information age, we prize critical thinking. The ability to logically compare different ideas and outcomes to solve problems is demanded and rewarded by our culture. Of course we want our children to be adept at critical thinking. But how do we model this vital skill? It's easy to assume we simply use hefty doses of criticism to impart this gift.

Here Mark and I hang our heads in shame because we were raised in critical households and instinctively thought we were doing our kids a favor by pointing out flaws. In a critical home, children flinch from the repeated barbs, under standards that seem unattainable, where every minor achievement is followed by "Yes, but ..." and how one could improve. Why would I lay this crushing burden on my own kids?

Of course, children need firm boundaries, and love must be tough, so what about constructive criticism? How else can children know the out of bounds unless we tell them? We may call it guidance or advice, but continual nagging can send a demoralizing message of general disapproval. This is never our intention.

Criticism is the dark side of our speech. It's a potent drug that should only be used with caution, carefully measured and surgically pinpointed on specific behavior: "Stop poking your brother." "It's time to share that toy." "I can't hear what you are trying to say because you are whining."

But global criticism, like global praise, is indiscriminate and blankets the child's soul with a discouraging label: "You are so mean." "You are being selfish." "What a baby you are, always whining."

These judgment calls are difficult to shake, especially from a parent's mouth. Like taking a Polaroid of our children, global criticism freeze-frames them in those unflattering moments and gives them the images to carry for future reference. These ugly photos can bully every other positive comment out of our children's minds.

What is really at stake? The child's feelings of worth.

IALAC

At the heart of all the words, words, words is the child's self-image. What picture of my child is being drawn through our conversations?

Jan Leonard was our real-life Mary Poppins, as Jon and Tim's first schoolteacher. In her preschool classes, she transformed her basement into a fun zone for the under five. But the biggest draw was her enthusiasm for little people, revealed by her twinkling blue eyes and perpetual smile. So when she asked all the parents to sit for a moment before school, we were attentive.

She didn't begin with the schedule or class rules, but with a story. (I later learned it was embellished from Dr. Sidney Simon's curriculum.) Imagine a large fragile cookie hung on a string around your child's neck with the letters IALAC. This cookie represents every child's initial appraisal of his or her life: I Am Lovable And Capable.

But life is not always gentle on cookies or children. Gradually, the different letters on this once-intact sign become chipped or have large bites removed: The father belittles his son for not catching the baseball; the mom calls her daughter a nuisance. The child wakes up one day no longer believing that he or she is worth loving, or the child sees himself or herself as inept—incapable.

Fortunately, these damaged cookies can be restored. The parent is the guardian of the IALAC sign and can make any needed repairs, especially if the parent is the one who bumped and cracked the letters.

This simple story gave us a visual of our sons' internal world. Whenever we sensed they were discouraged or upset, we could focus on those two big letters—Lovable, Capable—and build up those areas.

Both are necessary, like two sides of a ladder to which their self-image rungs attach:

- I can pile on the chores and expect excellence, to raise a highly responsible child, but does this little one only feel loved because of a great performance?
- I may interpret love as doing everything for my child, but my child's lack of responsibility leads to feelings of helplessness and takes a bite out of the *C*.

Every child needs to feel both cherished and responsible. Authentic love expresses both hugs and guidance. We can give our children affirmation as we push them out of the nest. We embrace and release.

Public Speaking

"What's it like to live in a fishbowl?"

We have been startled by this question from well-intentioned friends who see us and our children on public display. But certainly, every human life has an audience, and any child can be paraded in front of a crowd. Whenever a parent chooses a social setting to discuss a child, he or she has a megaphone.

Maybe it was because we did in fact live in a fishbowl of sorts that we became more sensitive to undressing our kids in public, not wanting to make them a topic of adult conversations—which inevitably, we did. So why do we brush past our own internal codes of honor as parents? Kid discussions are very contagious. Perhaps it's brought on by competition, to establish our children in the pecking order by comparison. Or sometimes we're looking for sympathy for a nagging frustration. And we always want to amuse our friends with the latest "You won't believe what my child did" tale.

But when we publicly describe our children, commenting on their behavior, good or bad, or relive events that belong to them, we border on objectifying their lives. Quick Facebook posts can allow anonymous strangers or friends to form unfair opinions about a toddler or teenager. Are we helping others see this child as a unique person? Or are we using our kids for some ulterior motive, to impress or avoid embarrassment, to complain or get a laugh?

This falls under the topic of manners, which are caught by example. We appreciate being asked if we want a story released to the public. So we can ask our kids too: "Would you mind if we told our friends about your role in the play?" "I would love to share about your funny episode at school. May I?"

Even better, we want to let our children tell their own stories. This is especially true if our children are standing next to us and we speak in the third person as if they were invisible: "He does this … enjoys that … wants to …"

To the child, it must feel like the times my parents would brag to their friends about my piano playing, insisting, "Play us a tune!" To my folks, it was a compliment, a chance for me to shine. But I only felt embarrassed to perform as if I were a sideshow that validated their parenthood.

Of course, the other extreme of bragging is public criticism. Sadly, some exasperated adults use bullying as a last-ditch effort to inspire change in their young. Mark and I have had a few parents drag a child to meet us only to confess their child's shortcomings—or "sins." The motives may be sincere: loving concern and a growing desperation to fix the perceived problem. But it is evidence of a serious breach in communication when we use an arena to heal a child's wound.

A public critique of our children always backfires—and ultimately drives us apart. If praise can be dangerous in public, how much more damaging is public criticism? As parents, we want to realize the untamed power of the tongue, to use it discreetly.

Learning a New Language

The love language in Mark's family was teasing. Mark sometimes wished he wasn't loved so much. Making fun of another person, especially a young one, is really emotional abuse. There is no joke if the joke's on you.

But this annoying humor was like breathing air, perfectly normal in that home. Family members routinely pointed out one another's obvious flaws. Unflattering stories were told and retold. Who needs entertainment if you can appoint a clown?

If this was our conversational heritage, it may take time to uproot this obnoxious plant. The best way to dig it up is to apologize to our children whenever we forgetfully tease. This lets everyone know this needling is not okay. Authentic parent-child relationships are built around mutual trust. We can all find laughs somewhere else.

My parents survived the Great Depression, so they knew how to pinch pennies; and they used language just as sparingly. It was rude to talk about yourself. You didn't comment on behavior that was expected. Affirming words were rarely spoken. Maybe once a year, my mom would take me aside and say, "You know that I love you. I don't say it very often, but I just wanted you to know." Among relatives, there were mostly handshakes instead of hugs.

Obviously, both of us faced steep learning curves for gaining a new parenting tongue. But as we practiced new ways of communicating, this foreign language became more natural than our native dialects. /// **THAT IS THE BEST NEWS FOR PARENTS: WE CAN, AT ANY AGE, LEARN THE LANGUAGE OF ENCOURAGEMENT.** /// As we practice, our kids will quickly pick it up too.

Words frame our day. They set the tone from our first "Good morning!" They seal the day with our last conscious thoughts.

Every night, our family ended with bedside prayer. This was more than a security ritual. It gave closure to the day and allowed both kids and parents to freely share any words that needed to be heard before eyes were closed. The dark room seemed a safer place to confide fears, ask an awkward question, or just reminisce about the best part of the day. This special time allows the child to speak and the adult to listen. The day's words often fail us, but we can hit review and delete at day's end and grow closer from our mistakes.

Knowing that we could finish the day with a good conversation, with God the Father listening, placed a quiet hug inside our souls. Then after a heartfelt snuggle and a forehead kiss, we were all ready for sleep. Tomorrow truly was a brand-new day.

Questions

How did your parents' words impact your life?

How can you specifically encourage your child this week?

Are you easily able to say "I'm sorry"? Why or why not?

If you're not easily able to say "I'm sorry," would you be willing to try it out this week?

Chapter 9

A BROKEN WOODEN SPOON

Adventures in Discipline

BY MARK

We are not necessarily doubting that God will do the best
for us; we are wondering how painful the best will be.
—C. S. Lewis

Jon the toddler hated naps. So every afternoon at one, we had a battle of wills. He would cry, "I don't wanna nap!" and thrash around in his bed. Then after we exited his room, we often heard the soft thud of his small feet hitting the floor to play with his toys.

After several rounds of placing him firmly back in bed, Jan grabbed a motivational tool: the wooden spoon. Waving it like a scepter, she threatened to give his chubby bottom a painful reminder if he sprung out of bed again. She left the room.

Thump. *Okay, that's my cue*, Jan thought. She reentered his room and, with added volume, said, "You have to nap—now!" She whacked the spoon on his dresser for emphasis, but to her surprise, the wood suddenly splintered in her hands.

They both stared in disbelief as her intimidating device was now in two. They both began to giggle, then howled hysterically. They finally ended up hugging each other as they laughed at the irony. Jon gave up and went to sleep, and we interpreted the moment as time to retire the spoon.

The broken spoon was a physical manifestation of our faltering strategy for discipline. The search was on to find better ways to shape our kids. Force alone did not work.

What Is Discipline?

Children don't come with manuals, so correcting our kids can be an ambiguously difficult assignment. Discipline is obviously more than painful correction or asking, "How do I make my child behave?" Discipline involves shaping the whole child into a responsible adult.

If our starting line is simply punishment, we are already behind in the game. *Discipline* actually means "to train." It is the root of the word *disciple*. So we're really talking about the discipleship of our children. Hopefully, 95 percent of our discipline will be this positive training, with barely 5 percent qualifying as the negative incentive. In that sense, this entire book is about disciplining our children and only a small part of this one chapter is about punishment. Without that intentional momentum, punishment could sadly eat up 95 percent of our focus.

Discipline is how our children learn right from wrong to develop inner character. Here is a glowing description from the Committee for Children about the purpose of discipline:

> To encourage moral, physical, and intellectual development and a sense of responsibility in children. Ultimately, older children will do the right thing, not because they fear external reprisal, but because they have internalized a standard initially presented by parents and other caretakers. In learning to rely on their own resources rather than their parents, children gain self-confidence and a positive self-image.[1]

The goal is not to create perfect little robots that obey our every whim. Our role as parents is to increasingly motivate our children to act from within, not simply act correctly. We don't want coercive obedience. Good behavior needs to be redefined as authentic choices that benefit our children and those around them. The finish line is to empower our children's *self-discipline*.

In early Scripture, the term "discipline" means "to dedicate a house or temple for a unique purpose" (see Deut. 20:5; 1 Kings 8:63). The Arabic equivalent means to rub the palate of an infant with chewed dates or oil to prepare the child to suck.[2] So discipline is really dedicating and preparing children for their life's purpose, helping them find a story bigger than themselves.

This is reinforced by the famous verse in Proverbs, "Train up a child in the way he should go, even when he is old he will not depart from it" (Prov. 22:6 NASB). As parents, we are called to *train* or *coach* our children toward *the way they should go*, that is, toward their purpose.

All children share a common call: to reflect the image of God, living as salt and light, shining His nature to others. That is the general *way* all children *should go*. But each child also has an individual calling and specific gifts. This is implied in the Hebrew: "… according to his or her *unique* way."[3] As parents, we can watch, learn, and help our children become who God has designed them to be. It's our calling to love, nurture, teach, and explain the good life—God's life. This means our discipline is a full-time job.

From our experience, Jan and I believe effective discipline uses the accelerator more often than the brake. If we create positive momentum in the right direction, we only occasionally need the negative braking. Discipline is not just a reaction to misbehavior; it's primarily proaction leading to positive behavior. No one wants to hear only what they've done wrong. Without encouraging forward motion, we quickly lose traction and the child will lose heart.

Everyday Discipline

Short cuts make long delays.

—J. R. R. Tolkien, *The Fellowship of the Ring*

Our children felt better about themselves when they took an active role. We saw our kids as response-able—capable of helping themselves and the whole family. We assigned age-appropriate chores from their earliest years. They began with picking up their toys.

When they could safely stand on a chair at the kitchen sink, they helped with dishes. They were allowed to sweep floors, wipe down bathrooms, and dust. We gave them white pillowcases, which they personalized, to hold dirty clothes and taught them how to wash, dry, and fold their own laundry.

Saturday was chore day, and we did fun and not-so-fun projects together, such as pulling weeds, painting the porch, and washing the car. Later in life, our kids took turns mowing the lawn. The work time preceded the playtime, another life lesson learned.

For all their efforts, we gave them each a small but meaningful allowance weekly, which increased with age. We made a chart of their week's work to display our expectations and their accomplishments as they crossed off finished chores. They were encouraged to save their hard-earned cash for bigger items on their wish lists.

We believed in delayed gratification. If they saw a toy they wanted, they had the ability to buy it if they patiently saved or waited for a birthday. This also required restraint on our part, to not intervene by buying the item for them so our kids would like us. What often happened was that prized toy would lose its luster after hours of hard work, so they were spared an impulsive purchase. They also learned the value of a dollar and to look for sales. They took better care of what they bought than the free gifts. Looking back, I also think this instilled more objectivity about possessions in our consumer culture.

/// JUST AS TRAINING OUR KIDS TO DO CHORES IS MORE DIFFI-CULT, NOT INDULGING OUR KIDS' TOY APPETITES REQUIRES DISCIPLINE FOR US PARENTS. /// It takes much more time and is messier to bake cookies with a toddler. Pulling out a credit card is simpler than watching our children count coins for weeks. But learning these life skills will ultimately improve the quality of everyone's life. Shortcuts often lead to very long roads in the end.

The most essential life skill Jan and I wanted to teach our kids was how to treat others well. Manners are how we express consideration for others. Being comfortable in our own skin is not antithetical to being polite. Like any language, being respectful is more easily learned when young.

Manners flow downstream from our own examples. That's why our kids need to be taught manners in a mannerly way. If we publicly interrupt our children to coach proper responses, it can be embarrassing and make everyone self-conscious. Instead, we can take our children aside or, better still, hold little rehearsals before the fact, practicing handshakes, looking adults in the eyes, or the protocol for introductions. Our pleases and thank-yous can be woven into everyday conversations.

Teaching our children grace is a daily discipline that can open enormous doors, just as the habit of rudeness can shut them tight. Taking the time to be mannerly will spare our children this hard lesson later in life. As Sheryl Eberly wrote, "Learning good manners will give your child essential tools for life."[4]

Learning through Play: Positive Discipline

Tim was an easygoing child but a picky eater. So we had the one-bite rule, adding that any complaints would result in more of the objectionable food. "Yay, broccoli!" was a common exclamation at the table and got the vegetable down. (Now more than all of us, he loves exotic foods.)

In shaping our kids, we can start with two questions: First, how do I think my child should behave in this situation? Second, how can I inspire my child to cooperate with that behavior? The direct "Do this, don't do that" approach often fails to positively motivate our children. Our kids learn best through play.

If our high watermark is enjoying our kids, then nurturing a close relationship through play will be essential to shaping their behavior. Through fun, they can acquire something as serious as good judgment.

We had contests for who could pick up the most toys. We pretended arms and legs were trains going through tunnels when getting dressed. Telling a story helped them sit quietly in the car. We made up silly songs as we did chores and did role reversals when a child whined about leaving the playground. The dreaded bath washcloth became a snuggly sea creature, toothbrushes could talk to little teeth, and sheets could be a land that needed clearing with a pillow mountain.

We tried to avoid using unrelated rewards, other than an allowance, for persuasion. What happens when a child outgrows that Popsicle treat or later in real life when rewards are often delayed or absent? We wanted our kids to connect their good actions to good consequences. Older children can understand reasons for limits and will work toward related long-range goals: "If you don't forget your lunch box all week, you can buy lunch on Friday." "If you help me build the fence, you can earn money faster for the bike." "I will listen, if you speak respectfully."

We tried to explain clearly the reasons for what we wanted our children to do. Beyond this, the best motivation was using their felt needs.

If they wanted to color in an expensive coffee table book, we gave them paper. When they didn't want to stop playing cars, we let each of them pick out one to go. If they didn't want to go to class, we listened.

Play and positive reinforcement create a bond that encourages cooperation. As we accept our children's invitations to enter their world, they are more eager to follow us into ours.

Discipline as Punishment

My grandfather had a framed set of old leather razor straps hanging on his wall. I'd always figured they'd been used for more than shaving, possibly to keep my dad in line. But only occasionally does discipline equal punishment in Scripture:

> Whoever spares the *rod* hates their children, but the one who loves their children is careful to discipline them. (Prov. 13:24)

> Folly is bound up in the heart of a child, but the *rod* of discipline will drive it far away. (Prov. 22:15)

> Do not withhold discipline from a child; if you punish them with the *rod*, they will not die. Punish them with the *rod* and save them from death. (Prov. 23:13–14)

Stern disciplinarians are eager to quote these verses, which are certainly recorded for our insight. But only those who are positively training their kids have earned the right to use them. And they need some further explanation.

Discipline as punishment is reserved for those rare moments of defiance, when our children have clearly heard and understood our requests, boundaries, or rules and have marched on to defy us. They have deliberately crossed an obvious line.

Jan and I were the last generation raised under corporal punishment. Spanking with a wooden spoon, paddle, belt, or flyswatter would qualify to sting the bottom but hopefully not cause physical damage. Even public schools in the '50s and '60s had paddles hanging ominously in the vice principal's office. But in the '70s, it was up for discussion. Behavioral studies began, and books for and against were being written.

At first, Jan and I interpreted the "rod" of Scripture literally, using a wooden spoon to sting the upper thigh. Books advised parents never to touch the child with the hand but only with an object that they would grow to respect. We were ready with our symbol of authority, but we were naive about the complexities.

Two-year-old Jon had been warned not to touch the stone fireplace hearth, indicating that it was "Hot, hot, hot!" The command was for his safety since we often lit cozy fires.

I took Jon over to the hearth with spoon in hand, saying, "No, hot," and waved my instrument of power. It worked. He understood; at least I thought he did.

A few days later, he sauntered over to the hearth and looked back at me. Our eyes met as I tilted my head to let him know I was watching. He then reached out his chubby little hand as if to touch it, and I warned, "Jon!" He turned as if to walk away from the fireplace but not before he purposely brushed his diapered rear against the forbidden stone. Was that an infraction? He technically hadn't touched it; his diaper had. I was being tested. Game on.

We eventually learned that discipline was more than warnings and threats with a wooden spoon. It involved praise for honoring boundaries and assurance that rules were for their benefit, not for arbitrary reasons. But our biggest disciplinary tool was always our relationship with our kids; it was who we were, not what we carried. How we loved our sons, the time we spent together, and modeling the behavior we expected were so impactful that punishment was not the central issue.

Those who still insist we interpret the "rod" literally may not fully understand the term. The rod was a shepherd's tool, a two- to four-foot club used primarily as a weapon to ward off predators. The hooked staff, on the other hand, was used to guide the sheep. No shepherd would ever beat his own flock with a rod.

So these verses are not an invitation to physically harm our children, but to discipline them in every way, including punishment. In fact, there is now substantial research showing that physical punishment can make children more defiant and aggressive in their adolescent years.[5] Not all parents administer corporal punishment calmly, with just a harmless sting. Too often anger is driving the correction. We are charged to guide and protect our children as their shepherds. The rod, then, becomes a figurative term for appropriate and loving correction in the hands of a kind parent.

There are many hot fireplaces in life that we want our kids to avoid. Like experienced guides, we can show them the way around. Our instructions should be clear and lovingly reinforced. The hopeful outcome is a confident, responsible adult who is comfortable setting their own boundaries and shepherding others.

Both Needed: Truth and Love

We believe the words *truth* and *love* form the parameters of God's discipline. Or as Ephesians 4:15 says, "… speaking the truth in love." We need love and truth to adequately shape our children, just as God's approach with us includes both.

Truth, or in the Hebrew language *faithfulness*, indicates reliability regarding expectations. We do what we say, and we expect the same from our children. Our kids need parents who will set clear boundaries and hold the line of truth. Reliable parents can be trusted. This faithful truth was at the center of ancient Jewish community. It's a critical aspect of discipline in our homes as well.

Love is the other side of the coin. This warm, affirming attention is an essential player alongside a parent's demands or *truth*. These parents are lovingly responsive and involved in their children's lives. Both the parents and the children will make mistakes, but "love covers a multitude of wrongs" (my adaptation of 1 Peter 4:8).

Studies have actually measured these qualities in families. Parents who are lovingly involved with their children and also hold the line of truth with appropriate boundaries have more cooperative and capable children. But the lenient best-friend parents or the harsh drill sergeants tend not to have well-adjusted children.[6]

The beauty is in the balance. Love and truth are not contradictory; we need both. /// TRUTH AND LOVE TOGETHER ARE HOW GOD RAISES HIS KIDS AND SHAPES OUR LIVES (JOHN 1:14). ///

What difference does our discipline style make? The benefits of *loving and truthful* parenting, as well as the harmful effects of indulging or harsh parents, are apparent in early preschool and continue through adolescence into adulthood. How we choose to discipline leaves a lasting impression on our kids. We must shepherd our children with both love and truth.

The Parable of Dimetapp

Things aren't always as they appear. It would be easy if discipline, punishment in particular, were cut and dry, black and white, but it is nuanced in ways unimaginable. Discipline is not for the faint of heart.

Jon had an ear infection when he was not quite four. It was a cold, snowy winter night. He was wearing blanket sleepers, huggable red Pooh Bear pajamas that I wished he would never outgrow. We had given him medicines before putting him in bed. One of them was Dimetapp. It promised to relieve congestion and had a pleasant grape flavor and color that made it acceptable to kids. Jon slurped it down and went quickly to sleep.

Around 11:00 p.m., I awoke with the feeling that someone was staring at me. Opening one eye, I was startled to see it was true. Jon was standing on my side of the bed with his eyes twelve inches from my face. I quickly leaped out of bed, hugged Jon, and carried this fuzzy red Pooh Bear back to his den.

"What's wrong?" I whispered, not wanting to wake Jan. He simply answered that he couldn't sleep. I told him it was nighttime and we all needed to sleep. I patted his back until he dozed off.

I returned to bed, quickly falling into dreamland. It wasn't quite 1:00 a.m. when I was startled again by Jon's staring face. This time I wasn't so gentle. I whisked him into my arms and said firmly, "C'mon, Jon, you need your sleep. What are you doing?" He sheepishly replied, "I can't sleep."

Once again I tucked him in and patted his back until he fell asleep. Exhausted and now paranoid, I retreated to my covers. This was becoming a long night.

It wasn't even thirty minutes before I again heard the pitter-patter. Pooh Bear was becoming bouncy Tigger, returning to haunt my dreams. Jumping out of bed, with obvious irritation, I blurted out, "What is going on? Why won't you sleep? It's nighttime!" I was both commanding and pleading with little Pooh, begging him, "Please, just let me sleep."

We survived that night, but the next one was torturously the same. My thoughts held running conversations: *What can I do? Should I discipline him? Does he need to be punished? He's only four. He hasn't been out robbing neighbors in the night. He's simply ruining my sleep. What is causing this misbehavior?* I was at my wits' end.

Like a detective, I combed through details of the last couple of days to find what was different. Why would Jon suddenly change his sleeping habits and want to stare at me all night? Then I spotted something new in his routine—the Dimetapp! I quickly read the side effects, which included nervousness and anxiety, and the description fit Jon perfectly. That night we eliminated the purple syrup, and we both slept like babies.

Discipline is not as easy as following a recipe in a cookbook. The variables are many. We need to know our ingredients to be able to improvise.

Baking a Good Cake

Through trial and error, Jan and I gradually identified several key ingredients for administering punishment well. Like a balance of flavors, if we eliminate certain ones, the final product will taste horrible. We sadly remember times when our quick reactions left a bad taste in everyone's mouth.

Effective discipline first adds positive ingredients to the mix: quality time, patience, good examples, creative momentum, and encouragement—all topics in our previous chapters. Only in this loving context can we introduce punishment. Punishment is that needed pinch of salt, but too much ruins the cake.

Here are some necessary elements that comprised our salty discipline:

1. Establish clear limits and appropriate boundaries. This initial step is where misbehavior can be uprooted before it takes over the child's day. Like a shoe that fits perfectly, setting rules that match our children to their circumstances is necessary. Human life demands order, and boundaries protect that freedom. But they can be kept at a minimum because guidelines are for our children and not the reverse.

We want to set thoughtful, realistic boundaries. Does my ten-year-old need to keep her hair brushed for her own safety—or to avoid my embarrassment? Is it worthwhile to force my imaginative child to completely clean his room every day, ripping up the pretend worlds he has built? Sometimes, we need to move boundaries that we want but aren't working for our children. If we set the bar too high, the child will lose heart; too low, and the child won't rise to the occasion.

Every boundary must be clearly stated if we want our children to cooperate. This seems obvious, but do our kids really hear our communication? When Jon and Tim were playing intently, they often didn't respond to my voice. So I made sure they looked at my face when I spoke, then had them repeat my instructions. Until I heard the echo, I knew they hadn't heard. They were rarely defiant but often busily deaf. We can even practice setting boundaries as we play with our children: Mother May I, board games, and reversing roles all can teach kids about limits through fun means.

Sometimes as parents we don't feel like maintaining our fences. But consistency is the magic ingredient for reinforcing our expectations. The circumstances, our emotions, and children's moods will vary, but rules that change with the weather are assumed unimportant. From the child's point of view, his or her resistance with whining might change the parent's mind. Or our child might condition us to repeat our commands nineteen times, and will stall until nineteen. If we hold the line early with clear, fair boundaries, it will help with cooperation later on.

When our two sons were young, we taught them not to run into the street but always wait for us, look both ways, and only cross when the light turned green. It was life or death. Now older, they thankfully cross on their own, still looking both ways and waiting for green.

Our rules are renegotiated as our kids grow up. In fact, we want them to internalize our guidance so we are not the eternal enforcers but they own that wisdom behind the rules and are self-regulated. Boundaries exist for our children, and when they have outgrown them, we have accomplished the goal.

2. Know your child. We noticed that our children's behavior was largely shaped by their physical, emotional, and social well-being. When a child can't obey because of some overriding weakness, any punishment may be unfair. Is my child tired or hungry? Has another kid been a bully? Is my child's love tank low? These questions seem extraneous to the stern, quick-to-punish parent. But there's no point in dousing a flame without cutting the fuel supply. Misbehavior usually points to something a child wants to gain, such as attention, an object, power, peer approval, or even love. We also need to be realistic in knowing that children behave like, well, children.

We had recently moved and enrolled Jon in a new kindergarten. When he came home, he started picking on Tim. This wasn't typical Jon, and we couldn't identify the source of his misbehavior. So Jan followed Jon to school and noticed a classmate was sticking pins through the toes of his tennis shoes to poke the new kid, Jon. What won't bullies think of? Jon, of course, was displacing his anger onto his younger brother. The issue was not simply Jon's misbehavior but the important context of the classroom bully. It never hurts to step back and ask what's happening around the child.

Children's various temperaments need to be handled differently too. One of our sons was more easily steered than the other. A strong-willed child may need extra firmness but should not be discouraged from being tenacious. As C. S. Lewis stated, "Our Lord finds our desires not too strong, but too weak."[7] That strong child might be the next president, world champion, or Michelangelo. Our discipline is part martial arts, where we learn to channel our child's challenging strength toward leadership and solid character. Those powerful wants come from our child's heart, which we never want to break.

Compliant children need gentle encouragement and may need only a stern look to change their behavior. They do express themselves, but more softly. They may act out differently, carrying their struggles inside. These children need extra time for sensitive listening, to prime the pump to hear their quiet hearts.

3. Know yourself. When my kids misbehave, I need to examine my life too. Am I distracted? Are they just pushing my buttons—and what are those buttons? Do I need to set new boundaries or move one? Have I focused only on their negative behavior, not praising them for the good? Are their love tanks low? Ultimately, I need to ask if this is a battle of wills or a battle within me. Maybe my kids have just absorbed my bad mood.

Our children behave differently with each person. They quickly assess the person's assets and liabilities and strike a bargain to their advantage. Our young sons began to whine and cling when we arrived at a friend's house to pick them up. They had been playing happily for hours before we walked in. They knew how to pull our heartstrings, to maybe punish us for our absence or make up for lost attention. Somewhere along the way, they must have learned this behavior worked, so we wanted to stop any manipulation and hear what they were actually saying. It's helpful to identify our buttons before they get pushed.

We long for our kids to freely express emotions, but chronic whining, fits of temper, or destroying property go well beyond that sane line. We need to ask ourselves if we are somehow rewarding these unpleasant responses. What does the child hope to gain? Is there some basic need that is being frustrated? Even we parents can be nasty when expectations aren't met.

Just as a pilot anticipates a plane's performance under certain conditions, a parent is responsible for knowing the child's limits and potential for meltdown. We need to be forecasters of storms.

Dining out demanded this skill as we predicted long hours at the table with boring adult conversations. Jan packed a magic bag full of curiosities to last an hour, which hopefully would prevent food fights, sibling annoyance, and crawling under the table. I well remember one lunch at a waterside restaurant where the dining experience outlasted Jon's and Tim's attention spans. They were released to explore the beach, but we soon spotted them bodysurfing fully clothed in the Chesapeake Bay. Why were we surprised?

Time warnings also anticipate our children's emotional attention spans, allowing them to adjust to our expectations. Kids can't turn a quick corner when engrossed or having a fabulous time. Who wants to end the party? But we can break the bad news slowly: "I'm giving you a heads-up. We are leaving in fifteen minutes, and I'll need you to start picking up your toys in ten minutes. So have fun, but get ready to leave." Then at ten minutes another warning, followed by "Leaving in five minutes." This allows our children to prepare for the inevitable, to play quickly with a neglected toy and get ready to obey. Kids need steps to manage their disappointment. If I don't adequately communicate, how can I punish my child for an abrupt transition?

There are good coaches, not just good players. I couldn't simply expect my kids to be better players. I wanted to be a better coach, learning all the techniques available.

4. Focus on the behavior and match the punishment. It's not always easy, but we must keep our eyes on our child's behavior, not the intent. Our overmoralizing makes an unfortunate choice worse by focusing on the child personally, not what has been done. I can talk about the lie without labeling my child a liar and discuss a thrown punch instead of calling my kid a bully. Names and labels are degrading weapons that border on emotional abuse.

When my child disobeys, it's not helpful to sermonize, calling the wrong a sin or to induce guilt, saying, "How does Jesus feel about this?" This is not the great white throne of judgment. The child is not functioning at an adult level. The kid just wanted to play longer or keep the toy. To magnify the bad choice into something more serious does more harm and risks shaming the child, who now might believe he or she is an evil person. Sadly, this manipulative language can be used by us adults who want to win by belittling or flashing a God badge.

We can treat each infraction as its own unique event. Certainly we don't want to judge the character of our child as being forever a certain way. That puts a permanent frame around the failure. Our children are like warm clay, so our words or attitudes can mold them into what we actually fear.

Before we administer any appropriate punishment, we want to slow everything down. Time is our friend. We can allow emotions to cool, get all the facts, listen, and discuss with our mates, if available. It's helpful to play out the possible consequences in our minds to see if they feel right. Then the less emotional parent can dispense the punishment. Unjust punishment is impossible for a child to understand, especially when falsely blamed. /// **WE KNEW WE WOULD MAKE MISTAKES, SO IF WE HAD TO ERR, WE WANTED TO ERR ON THE SIDE OF MERCY.** ///

It's always best if consequences for disobedience are spelled out beforehand, when we set the boundary. Then our children already know what is coming. But many times, we need to make it up in the moment. That's why a cool down is important; because it keeps us from serving our child a month of punishment for stealing a paper clip. We want any painful correction to fit the crime. It's especially useful if the discipline is related to the wrong: "You broke the vase after being told not to throw the ball in the house. Now you need to clean up the mess and buy another vase with your own money."

Time-outs can be a useful "rod." They provide a painful loss of activity, making our children more aware of their behavior, without causing physical pain. But time-outs given in public, especially in front of other children, can be quite shaming. We should use them discreetly and only for short periods.

A restriction is a longer time-out, usually for older children. Jan and I were not fans of restrictions because they often punished our whole family, especially if one child was kept from a preplanned, fun family event. It's also very difficult to know what is fair in length or type of restriction. Was it too much or not enough? Ideally, as with time-outs, it can be linked directly to the misbehavior. A restriction from peers or activities is appropriate if one of these was the catalyst for the bad choice.

Discipline can also be fun. We played a dinner game called Cave Man to teach our sons to use eating utensils, not their fingers. When they became involved in conversation, they sometimes forgot and grabbed food with their hands. Anyone who spotted these primitive manners could shout, "Cave man!" The offender had to leave the table and count out loud to one hundred before he could return to eat in a civilized way. One child had to leave the room eight or nine times in one night—hilarious! Clearly, this was not behavior that demanded formal punishment but could be altered through play.

5. Reality discipline. For us, the most effective way to deal with misbehavior was using the present circumstance to teach our kids. Called reality discipline, it uses a creative approach to punishment that teaches responsibility.[8] It makes our children responsible for their choices by letting them experience the natural consequences of their behavior. Jan and I realized that the harsh realities of life accomplished what repeated time-outs and stings on the thigh could not.

Too often as parents, we shield our kids from built-in ramifications, not allowing them to learn from their mistakes and grow. But real life has an effective reward and punishment system. Our kids can, and will, reap what they sow. Better to learn this lesson early.

If one child ate candy he was supposed to save, he wouldn't enjoy it later with his sibling. When a child refused to eat supper with the family but later wanted a private meal, he was consoled and loved but sent to bed with hungry consequences.

Jon's most painful lesson came after he bought his own new bike at eleven. He wanted to ride by himself to the corner doughnut shop and I agreed, only warning him to lock his bike. He didn't use the lock, and his new bike was stolen. I anguished over whether to rescue him. Was I too hard on him? It was hard on me not to intervene in this painful lesson. But eventually, my reluctance to fix the problem gave the story a better ending.

A month later, a gentleman in our church heard about the loss and bought Jon a bike. I decided it was just like God to allow grace to step in. Weeping endured for the night, but joy eventually showed up.

Reality discipline gives our kids choices. Instead of commanding them to mow the lawn or else, we let them know they can play with friends after they cut the grass. The lawn will eventually get mowed because they choose to play later. This freedom of choice is empowering for the child, instead of feeling boxed in by punishment.

When we give our kids legitimate choices, they will own the dilemma and want to solve the tension. This is also great training for solving problems later in life.

6. Avoid conflict, if possible. None of us as parents should go looking for a fight. If we sense a showdown brewing, it's better to intervene early, provide an alternative, and redirect our children's energy. Like playing chess, we need to look ahead a few moves to win. Jan and I especially tried to stay several steps ahead of our very young kids. Changing a situation can prevent our children from inappropriate actions. Taking the path of least resistance is sometimes the wisest way out.

We never want to set up children to fail by giving commands they can't emotionally or physically follow. That's like walking our kids into a candy story, then scolding them for wanting to buy some. It's unfair to offer choices to our children that aren't genuine or allow them to choose what we can't allow in the end.

If specific poor behavior is being repeated, it's helpful to look at the bigger picture. What could be triggering this response? Rather than confronting the battle with a war, we can try to get to the root issue. Showdowns are painful for everyone; some are unavoidable, but many can be averted with practical adjustments. Wise parents avoid the edge. And of course, we parents can have meltdowns too!

7. The setting for punishment: in private. Punishment makes a child feel bad; it can be unintentionally shaming. So whenever possible, we can save our children's dignity by correcting them in private. Our tone is also important; we should never demean or belittle our children.

I appreciate how Jesus handled discipline in Matthew 18. There are several steps to follow, beginning with utter privacy, which eliminates public shame. The same tender God gave the first couple fig leaves. Right behavior is only a means to the greater end of love and truth. I often want to attack the situation first with abrupt, quick hands, but correcting my child is a delicate art.

8. Loving affirmation follows correction. After any punishment, a child needs to be embraced with affirming words of love. Our children want reassurance that our relationship is unchanged because nothing can make us love them more or any less. We can tell them how much they mean to us and we will always cherish who they are.

If we disciplined with harsh words or overreacted, this is an excellent time to admit it, without apologizing for the boundary. Our kids won't learn good behavior if we have behaved badly, but they absorb volumes from our honest confessions and are more apt to change their behavior too. This may be when the precocious child tries to lessen the sentence through tears. Although this may pull on our hearts, we must stay strong and defend our line of truth, in love.

Discipleship Is the Big Picture

I think of Jesus's comforting words to Peter on the beach, after the apostle had denied Him three times. He pulled Peter aside, so only

John heard their private conversation. Peter's crime was appalling. To counter Peter's three hurtful denials, Jesus gently coaxed him to make a threefold confession of love. Then He said, "Get back to work as the shepherd I called you to be." No scolding, no lectures, no shame. Correction done, forgiveness given, with an eye on the big picture of discipleship: truth and love.

Our words can heal our children's sad hearts. This also reminds us of the prodigal's father, who ran to embrace his returning wayward son. All is forgiven. Let's celebrate! Truth and love stand beautifully together in this picture of reconciliation. Truth and love can change your child, your family, and eventually, the world.

Questions

How would you describe your discipline style? Do you err on the side of love as a pushover parent or on the side of truth as a strict disciplinarian? Or are you a mixture of both? Explain.

Is there a reoccurring problem over which you are struggling with your child?

Is there a different strategy you can use to improve this situation?

In which new area can you positively discipline or train your child? Write down your thoughts.

Chapter 10

THE COMPANY WE KEEP

The People Who Matter Most

BY JAN

> *You are the same today as you'll be in five years except for two things: the books you read and the people you meet.*
> —Charlie "Tremendous" Jones, *Life Is Tremendous*

Packing for our West to East Coast move meant pawing through eight years of history. A friend who was helping kept holding up odd items, photos, and other memorabilia, asking, "Is this significant?" That is our ongoing dilemma with people, sorting through our accumulated relationships to safeguard those most meaningful to us.

These are the people who matter most. They matter not only to us but also to significant others in our inner circles. They are the influencers, the encouragers, those with the loudest voices. Or they are a fragile, uniquely dependent, necessary part of your life. You would take a bullet for them, and their calls regardless of the hour.

Unique relationships—we all have them. They are peculiar to us because they arrived on our doorsteps: a spouse, child, parent, or friend with history. But can we also cultivate friendships intentionally? This question becomes especially important as we have children and include folks who will shape them. These significant people will leave lasting impressions on our kids, beyond music lessons or choosing the right schools.

Jesus's relational style created concentric circles of friends, increasing in size, starting with the few, the dozen, the seventy, the dozen times ten, followed by everyone else. He focused most of His time on the first and second groups: close friends Peter, James, and John, and the handpicked twelve.

Why would the world's most influential leader waste so much time on this tiny group? He knew His humanity. He realized that as a human, He was confined to only one place at a time. If He spread Himself thinly and failed to nurture these few friends, the impact of His life would be correspondingly shallow. Even God as man knew His limitations and chose wisely.

The Inner Circle

Parents have only a few short years to make a difference in a few lives. We can't afford to give many people precious quality time, but we can focus on nurturing a handful of significant others. These are the ones who are uniquely grafted into our lives, and we in theirs. This modest group always includes immediate family when we become parents: our spouse and our kids. That defines our first inner circle.

But there is one caveat: Sometimes the inner circle changes dramatically because one parent dies or moves away. Or our nuclear families mutate into dangerous forms and we need to redefine our closest relationships—an abusive spouse or a dishonest relative can't be trusted. All relationships are complicated, but those closest to us can be especially confusing. Sadly, sometimes the most natural fit for a close tie needs to be distanced.

Roughly half of all marriages in the United States end in divorce, leaving one-third of the children living without a dad and another five million without a mom.[1] Because these nurturing bonds are unraveling in our culture, it is even more vital that kids experience safe, healthy relationships. All parents, married or single, must be gatekeepers for all the folks who could influence their kids' lives—especially in the early years.

Every family is actually a miniature community. It's a relational ecosystem that needs protection as well as space to breathe and grow. I recently read through my old journal entries, and the experience reimmersed me in the intense pressures of my twenties and thirties. No one raises a family in a petri dish, but we all struggle to survive in germy, shark-infested waters, trying to stay afloat in strong ocean currents. Our environment is anything but family friendly. To thrive, we must find and hold our place in this ever-changing, sometimes-hostile climate.

The Inner Circle: Marriage

We were fortunate; our parents gave us a primer on how a healthy inner circle lives and breathes. They were inseparable in their commitments. Mark's parents also were famous for their public disagreements, but we always knew they had each other's backs. In both marriages, no person or circumstance could break that loyalty.

They were best friends. They ran dual errands just to keep each other company. They planned vacations together. Our moms had special dates with friends, and our dads worked long office hours, but they were inseparable most nights. They often joked about "spoiling each other rotten."

We realize there are many models for marriage: the wife works full-time while the husband raises the kids, or both have careers and separate bank accounts, or the home responsibilities are split so that both can pursue a calling together. But the giant lesson we watched unfold in our parents was that their marriages came first, ahead of children, hobbies, careers, and close friends. Every other duty or pleasure was a distant subordinate. Mark's folks spoke often about guarding their inner circle and lived that ideal for sixty-five years until Doreen went to be with Jesus. My parents are still going strong after seventy-three years together.

If we are married, the most beneficial example for our child is nurturing our relationship with our spouse. I was given a basket with violet plants right before a two-week vacation. When we returned, only the basket had survived; the plants were completely brown. Unfortunately, it was too late to revive the brittle stems.

Our most significant relationships need regular watering of time and focused attention. Otherwise, we will wake up to only a shell with little life inside. Every marriage is a living organism that requires nutrients to survive. Our need for human touch does not cease when we outgrow infancy; it continues as adults. To thrive, we need authentic love, just like we need water and air.

Nurturing our marriage wasn't natural or easy at first. Mark was consumed with caring for others as a new pastor and said yes to almost every need. I felt neglected, so I made an appointment to see him—which he canceled! My resentment kept snowballing into monstrous expectations. We were treating our relationship casually and took each other for granted.

We began with a baby step in the right direction, establishing a date once a week. It wasn't much of an adjustment, just a few hours, but it signaled something important: our marriage mattered. We recruited a sitter, got the kids fed and in pajamas, and left the house together as two adults without kids. This is no small feat, as any young parents will admit. But we blocked off one night every week, week after week.

Couples need this regular time alone to remember why they liked each other in the first place. Otherwise, we reduce our marriages to functional roles and can wind up groveling in our separate corners instead of partnering in life.

Initially our date night conversations were not helpful: reporting on a child's hard day at school or problems with an employee at work or balancing the checkbook. How romantic. Eventually we had a revelation: we needed two separate time commitments in the week, one for practical details of schedule and problem solving and the other for companionship. We had been using our date night to dump our garbage, which was a definite need, but it ruined our romance.

So we created another moment in our week when we could bring our lists and pencil in the calendar. One was utilitarian, the other, strictly relational—no dumping allowed. This simple pattern has helped us grow together, not apart. And after forty-two years, over five hundred months of date nights have kept the plant watered.

Still, we've had to fight for our marriage in adverse climates. We've experienced the equivalent of earthquakes, sinkholes, hurricanes, and droughts. But honestly, most of our tensions came from within, arising from differing expectations: "I thought you would be available to watch the kids." "I wanted you to go with me tonight." "Why is that bill overdue?"

We already know what we want, and we expect the other to sign our invoice. That's why the nonromantic weekly strategy time can be a marriage saver. We can both play our hands and realize which cards don't fit. If one of us is out four nights in a row, then do we want to have friends over the remaining evenings? Since one person is facing a deadline, the other can be more time sensitive. If parents are arriving next week, we can work together on cleaning the house and clearing our schedule.

We are searching for the "win-win," not an "I win; you lose" scenario. If one of us consistently loses, then we will both lose in the end because one of us has shrunk. /// **A MARRIAGE NEEDS BOTH PEOPLE TO BE FULLY PRESENT TO THRIVE.** ///

It's true: we can't change another person. But in fact, we will become different people over time, just as our physical bodies exchange old cells for new. If we remain close and keep talking, we will be able to accept and adapt to this inevitable change instead of growing apart. We can even become each other's cheerleaders for trying something new.

Speaking of new, any break in routine is like a minivacation. It can reset the marriage template to simple enjoyment of each other. Sometimes the most practical thing we can do for each other is to be impractical.

Why is romance essential to parenting? Our marriage can be a model for our kids' future relationships. Two parents can provide the laboratory for children to observe, test, measure, hear, and feel what love looks like. They will carry this qualitative insight into their own marriages or friendships. And the world will thank you.

Here lies a delicate balance. The inner circle includes the kids, so there is a subtle tendency to build our marriage around them. That is like building a house without a floor. /// IF WE ARE BLESSED TO HAVE A LIFE PARTNER, THAT LOVE BECOMES THE FOUNDATION FOR THE OTHER RELATIONSHIPS IN THE HOME. ///

A Smaller Inner Circle: The Single Parent

Some of the finest parents we know are slugging it out solo. What a challenge to be two people in one, or not see your children for set times. For the single parent, widening the circle to include significant people is especially vital.

Ideally, but not always easily, a single parent can find friendships with quality two-parent families. This allows the single parent's children to have an example of marriage in their lives. The child can also spend time with a role model for the absent dad or mom. These caring friends can give the exhausted parent a needed break.

Since approximately 35 percent of children in the United States live with only one parent, there is a great need for families with both a mom and a dad to include these children and parents in their extended families.[2] Single moms and dads are bravely trying to do what must seem impossible at times: give their children loving, secure, happy homes where they can grow. These smaller inner circles desperately need the encouraging presence of other families to keep thriving.

The Family Circle

Having time to simply be a small family unit is also essential. This is another balance beam for overcommitted parents to cross. One of our children's favorite moments was when we declared family time and made space for just us. Edith Schaeffer wisely said, "A family is an open door with hinges and a lock." We need both.[3]

We need time and space to connect without outside interference. This is how we deepen our roots and identity as a family. It's a social fact: we are different people when we are with others. Who are you really? Your child can find out when you close the door.

Also, who are *we*? What makes our family unique? Children want to know where they belong, to give their souls an address. Each family creates their own personality by spending quality time together. It builds an emotional shelter for children that satisfies their longing for security.

Our kids also respond to us differently when they are alone. You learn all kinds of important details: Their friend is having a birthday party, but they haven't been invited. Another friend has the stomach flu. They forgot to turn in that report. Maybe they could quit baseball and try tennis. Can you prove that God is real?

Susanna Wesley raised two of the most influential sons in the 1700s, John and Charles. They championed the First Great Awakening on the English side of the pond. Although nine of her nineteen children died young, she homeschooled ten children in extreme poverty and regularly scheduled an hour alone with each one to connect with them as individuals. Later John Wesley wrote, "I learned more about Christianity from my mother than from all the theologians of England."[4]

This one-on-one dynamic is vital to authentic relationship. We all crave focused attention, especially little people who look up to their moms or dads. This saturation of time spells out the child's value beyond words. Like date nights, regular solo moments with each child water the plant. /// CHILDREN NEED TO KNOW THEY BELONG BUT ALSO THAT THEY ARE UNIQUE, THAT THEY STAND OUT IN THE CROWD. /// Focused time does both: it builds security and self-worth. It lets kids know they matter.

The Vital Role of Extended Family

The next circle of trusted people *might* be the extended family. Again, for some parents, this is a selective process because healthier relationships may be found outside the bloodlines. A few stellar friendships can often be a better way to fill in this important group. As poet Robert Elliott Gonzales wrote, "A good many family trees are shady."[5]

We lived far away from extended family for most of our kids' lives. This was a loss because we lived separated from generations of great examples. But we found and adopted aunts, uncles, cousins, and grandparents whose lives were equally inspiring. We don't choose our relatives, but we are able to choose our extended families. There was Grandma and Grandpa Therkelsen who shared their wisdom, Mr. Maurice who taught piano riffs, the Polleys who supplied good movies, and the Clarks who showed our kids dance steps and soccer moves.

This is the best definition of extended family we can think of, stretching our walls to include an interesting assortment of caring friends. They were wild about our kids, and they enriched all of our lives immeasurably. Each person left a traceable deposit. We can still hear their voices: "Don't push your kids up a grade just because they're smart." "Expose your children to everything and be generalists in the early years." "Notice how your kids are manipulating you." "Expect the unexpected!"

We can't imagine raising our kids without them.

A Creative Community Expands the Horizon

Our children were cradled in a large community. This was about literally true for our firstborn, whose nursery was almost a conference center room. A dresser drawer, in a Spartan twelve-by-twelve dormitory space, was not my vision of a bassinet, but by moving to Lake Arrowhead eight months pregnant, it looked unavoidable. There were no available rentals on the mountain. I identified with Jesus's mother, Mary. Then on my due date, a small cabin mercifully became available within walking distance of the center. But the setting did not move. We were entrenched in community.

Looking back, this was an enormous plus. It set the tone for our family to have an open door when possible. We ate most meals (for free) at the crowded conference center where Mark worked, our babies passed to adoring faces. They were socialized by humanity in full force. We often invited students to hang out at our cabin, and the stream of people was like a life-giving tide, flowing in and out, reverberating off the walls of our tiny home.

What does a small child learn from this safe chaos? Community illustrates unique virtues: cooperation, patience, generosity, humor, and perhaps most of all, how to genuinely enjoy people. It also applies antivenom to our natural tendency to be selfish and live apart. What a gift this was to all of us, especially our children. We heartily endorse community for raising young humans.

Traveling minstrels still roam the countryside. Musicians, including songwriters, would frequently sit around our living room. All styles of music—folk, jazz, classical, bluegrass, and rock—would fill our home. This immersion in an artistic community had a profound impact on the open eyes and ears of our young. It put artistry within reach.

Our sons were given impromptu guitar lessons, learned the basics of recording, and overheard conversations about songwriting. Even their first demo tape was hand delivered to a record label by one of these artistic friends. The multiplied power of example shaped our children's early interests.

There were also visitors from other countries with thick accents. We served broken people at our table, or just friends of friends who needed a place to stay. We believe this varied fabric of humanity improved our kids' abilities to relate to all kinds of people.

When our kids were tiny, we invited a nationally known author for a home-cooked meal. He was seated where we usually placed baby Tim's high chair, and in my distracted serving, I accidentally tried to tie Tim's terry-cloth pig bib on this famous guest. At yet another meal, before dinner, I handed a paring knife to a TV show personality and asked if she would please finish chopping the vegetables while I ran my son to the ER for stitches. Inviting people into our homes does not mean they or we have to be polished and perfect.

We wanted to erase the usual walls that separate generations, eliminating the adult-versus-child categories, so we included our kids whenever possible with guests and let them color beside us at home gatherings. We wanted them to look adults (who were safe and friendly) in the eyes and not feel embarrassed by their small size. We believe this helped them feel they, too, played important roles in our community. Their voices counted.

Young children who are playfully thrown in the air and twirled around have better balance as adults. Maybe an abundance of healthy social stimulation allows kids to find their relational feet. Children's EQs (emotional quotients) are as critical to their future as their IQs. This ability to read people and serve them well can open more doors than academic success.[6]

The real genius of living closely with others is that children can experience more colors of personality in a safe environment. It expands their social genetic pool. Neither of us is highly organized or in love with details. But our kids had an adopted big brother who brought the elegance of order into their lives. Mark is a casual surfer, but another friend became a competitive surf coach. Another person is a wilderness guide and has shared with our sons his fascinating wildlife stories and enthusiasm for nature. Who would our kids be without all these amazing people?

Raising kids in the thick of community has its challenges because we are all flawed humans, sometimes clawing for survival in ugly ways. There are gentle, peaceful, humble people, and there are dangerously cruel people—and everything in between. Let's face it: Many adult issues are not suitable for children's tender hearts. So here is one final word about encouraging our kids to become acquainted with the human race: parental discretion is advised. In reality, true community can be a beautiful mess—just like us. But most of the time, it's just beautiful.

May God give back to you in love all the love you have given and all the joy and peace you have sown around you, all over the world.
—Mother Teresa, *In the Heart of the World*

Questions

Who are the people who matter most to you?

How can you make these people a priority in your life?

What relationships need to be nurtured?

What relationships need to be limited?

What relationships might need to be added?

Chapter 11
MYSTERY WAFFLES AND PADDLEBOARDS
Rituals and Relics

BY JAN

Families aren't easy to join. They're like an exclusive country club where membership makes impossible demands and the dues for an outsider are exorbitant.
—Erma Bombeck, *Family*

Almost every Saturday morning, Mark was in the kitchen. He was armed with a stovetop Belgian waffle maker and a recipe he had memorized with whipped egg whites, artery-clogging butter, and whole grain wheat flour. One morning, bored with the routine, he had an idea: let's play guess that flavor! He became the inventor of mystery waffles.

He separated the batter into four bowls and added unusual, secret ingredients into each, without letting us spy on the production. At breakfast, each waffle was sampled, and as the boys and I ate our fourths, we tried to guess the flavors. Was it Almond Joy, peanut butter, or pineapple and coconut? The delicious possibilities were endless. The first one to guess correctly was the winner of that round. It became our new Saturday morning ritual, lasting until junior high.

Sticky Practices

Our family traditions glue us together. These happy habits bring cohesion to our fragmented schedules and unite us after long hours apart. Far from obligations, they give us permission to do what we enjoy with those we love most.

Rituals build our kids' security, arranging predictable events that they can eagerly anticipate: Popsicles after school, making up stories in carpool, dancing before bedtime. Young children signal this need for repetition, beginning with being rocked back and forth. They demand the same story reread or a familiar toy carried around. This is how we learn life, by repetition and practice.

Our family customs allow us to celebrate our family-ness. They reassure our kids that they belong to our unique circle. We share fun family secrets with quirky routines that outsiders might not understand. We get the joke, the double meanings, the nuanced gestures—we get one another.

It's critical for a child's identity to have this safe place where they can be themselves and know where they fit. Honoring these special moments imparts value to our children, which in turn grows confidence for the world outside our walls. Deep roots can support towering trees.

This was the genius behind the feasts and days of celebration that God set up for His people. It created a life rhythm that brought the children and adults together at regular intervals to recall their history. God instilled these patterns into creation itself, with the movement of planets, seasons, even the daily rise and set of the moon and sun. We need this orderliness to regulate our own lives. It's empowering and comforting to a child to know what happens next.

Our unique family practices are like pleasant speed bumps that slow us down to remember who we are as a family. When the Israelites entered their Promised Land, they grabbed stones from the bottom of the Jordan River, which they had just miraculously crossed. Then they built a memorial to never forget that journey, God's faithfulness, and their distinct calling as God's family. We also need to grab stones along the way that connect our drifting lives, to remind us how we got here.

Our rituals celebrate and reinforce our values. From a deeply symbolic advent wreath at Christmas to frivolous game nights, we set aside time for what matters most: our beliefs, our history, and one another. This passes on to the next generation a rich family culture.

Rituals should be something we all look forward to doing. Both Mark and I had fathers who liked liver once a week. Eating liver every Friday is fine as long as everyone is excited about liver—we weren't. Mystery waffles were a good fit because we all liked waffles and friendly competition. Our night readings were also sacred. I don't know who enjoyed this ritual more, Mark or our sons. None of them could wait to dive back into some fantasy adventure of great writers, such as Tolkien or Lewis.

Our regular traditions should be easy and realistic. Can you really bake a seven-tiered cake once a week? Children especially enjoy simple pleasures, such as playing cards or singing together before a meal. The difference between an activity and a ritual is that the latter is easily repeated. If we're doing something often, we need to keep it practical.

We kept board games and puzzles in easy reach, nightly wrestling was a staple, and we were always ready for a quick round of flashlight tag. One night, when Mark was it, we snuck out of the dark house to the corner ice cream store. After he spent ten minutes in fruitless search, we phoned Mark to say where he could find us. His "prize" was buying everyone a cone.

Mark learned *The Third Man*'s theme song on piano for his grandfather before junior high. It was his grandpa's favorite tune, so Mark played it whenever he came over. This ritual got a second life in our home when it somehow became "The Bike Song." No matter what our kids were doing, the first piano notes had Jon and Tim running for their tricycles to ride wildly through the house. This fun musical punctuation also evolved into newly composed lion and crocodile songs, with accompanying costumes and animal imitations.

Our rituals combine who we are with what we like to do. We allowed bikes in the house and Mark was going to play the piano anyway. Why not create a fun memory? We can make rituals out of what we're already doing with some thinking outside the usual boxes.

These family practices do not need big time commitments and can be tailored to fit our lifestyles. We ate brown bread with baked beans and franks every Friday, adapting to New England culture, which was an excuse to eat food we all liked. We thanked God before meals with hands held, toasted punch cups of sparkling cider at holidays, and dragged out a bedraggled tissue clown head for birthdays, along with a red You Are Special plate.

We enjoyed game nights because they allowed us simply to be together in relaxed moments with no agenda. We made up competitions for everything, from egg-decorating contests to racing lobsters on the kitchen floor before we, gulp, boiled them.

Rituals can be woven easily into everyday necessities. /// **THE ENDANGERED FAMILY MEAL IS A POWERFUL SYMBOLIC TRADITION.** /// Sadly, just 40 percent of American families eat together regularly, but this was a stake we drove into the ground early.[1] Dinnertime together let us unwind after the day, sharing stories or new jokes and talking about tomorrow. The focus wasn't on the food, as in "Eat your vegetables or else," but on connecting. Nor was it a time to enforce formal table manners. We kept the atmosphere light and playful.

I planned meals everyone was enthused to eat: chicken and dumplings, salsa burgers, and I already mentioned the beans and dogs. We have to pick our battles, and table wars were not critical to our family's survival, but being together was. This was also not the time to discuss an unmade bed, deliver a homework lecture, or put pressure on one family member. We declared a cease-fire while we ate. This needed to be a safe time with no ambushes or complaining about one another. Many times, just sharing a meal resolved differences.

Soccer practice, school meetings, music lessons, and work schedules are often in conflict with eating together, but it's worth trying to maneuver around events to make it work as much as possible. Or maybe another meal, such as breakfast, makes more sense. If all else fails, we can make banana splits before we collapse after the day's activities.

When we ate our food, we fasted from technology. The TV was silent, and calls went to voice mail. When dining out, it's become normal to see an entire family of five all interacting with their smartphones, not speaking to one another. That doesn't count for a shared feast.

Meals that involve the whole family are especially engaging. One sets the table, another stirs while someone else chops, and we all clean up together afterward. There are fewer complaints about food choice when each of us has a hand in preparation. Kids are always more appreciative of food they have made. It is *our* family meal.

For us, meals were also good times to hear fascinating stories from an older family member: how my father grew up visiting his grandfather, Daddy Mac, who bred Tennessee walking horses for traveling ministers; Mark's dad was the youngest civil engineer hired in Santa Ana; Mark's mom was drum majorette for the Montebello marching band; and my mom was a traveling nurse during World War II. This storytelling connects us to the fascinating people behind the photos.

Another daily necessity for families is bedtime. Nighttime rituals are especially important to children before they experience the inevitable dark separation from parents. These consistent patterns allow children to wind down emotionally after an exciting day. We began our nightly routine with the bath.

It was hard to get our kids into the warm water, but even harder to get them out of that wet imaginary world. So we made a fun ritual out of exiting the tub: Mark invented cold water bombs and found another use for our kids' little green plastic army men. After the ten-minute warning, the green men would invade as paratroopers into the tub, as Mark dropped them over the shower curtain. This was only the first wave of attack, however. He then filled an eight-ounce cup with cold tap water and randomly poured it on their heads from above. They slithered, laughing, to escape from the shock, and eventually surrendered by flying out of the tub. It was a memorable way to force-quit a bath.

/// **OUR BEDTIME CEREMONY INCLUDED READING A FAVORITE STORY, CUDDLY HUGS, TALKING ABOUT THE DAY, AND PRAYING TOGETHER.** /// We sang to our very young children. We tried not to rush this time but make it the priority it really is. We especially thanked God for all the special people in our lives. Then we gave our kids one last "I love you" or "You're the best" or "I want to grow up and be like you" affirmation. Then lights went out.

All kids are skilled at sabotaging bedtime rituals with evasive techniques, from crying for water to insisting they see something scary in the corner or they need to use the potty one last time. We can be loving and firm about keeping that sleep time in place. If we reward any of their tactics, it will only prolong the agony the next night. This is a test; it is only a test.

The Paddleboard

A twelve-foot mahogany paddleboard hangs on our family room wall above our heads. It is a silent reminder of our California heritage. It was built by Mark's grandfather and dad from a diagram published in the July 1937 issue of *Popular Mechanics* magazine.[2] We have black-and-white 1940s pictures of his grandparents posing on the board and home movies of Mark's folks paddling in Newport Beach Back Bay before it was civilized. Our family took turns surfing on the paddleboard at our local beach before we hung it on our family room wall. Mark rescued this wooden relic from becoming two halves when his mom wanted a luau table for the patio. Sure, it's valuable, but its real worth to us is that it embodies our early West Coast history that will hopefully be passed along to our grandkids.

Family keepsakes remind us of our unique history: the teapot my grandmother brought over from Sweden when she was young; the large Sallman print of Christ knocking at the door that hung in my grandparents' entry and now hangs in ours; the black-and-white photos of assorted relatives who rode a buckboard to Anaheim Landing beach; the pump organ that traveled from Lake Michigan to Israel, then California, that still smells like my grandparents' basement.

Like old photos that display family resemblance, these relics from another generation place our family in a bigger story. And that's the point. They plant our kids on a longer timeline in an ever-changing world. In a society that quickly scraps the old for the modern, they provide continuity, instilling a respect for the family history.

Our children barely knew their surviving great-grandparents, let alone the great-greats, who experienced the Dust Bowl in Oklahoma or became cowboys in Texas. But the framed original land grant reminds them of that rugged existence. These colorful stories shape our kids' identities by connecting them to their ancestors. They can build on their qualities, like cathedrals that span generations to complete.

Keepsakes help children recall their own personal histories: rock collections, artwork, photo books, or beloved toys. Our grandson now enjoys the Hardy Boys collection that his dad, Tim, read at his age. We can't save every stuffed dolphin we bought at the marine park, but we can isolate and preserve the real treasures of exceptional moments.

All these rituals and relics deepen our family bonds. They vaccinate our kids against the epidemic of narcissism in our culture. They remind us all that life did not begin, nor will it end, with us. /// EVERY FAMILY NEEDS AN APPRECIATION FOR THEIR UNIQUE HISTORY, AS WELL AS EXCITEMENT FOR WHAT'S NEXT. ///

These milestones were obviously important for us because we moved eight times before our kids were in high school. But really, every family needs these bearings because our whole civilization is relocating at rapid speed. The new and improved is obliterating the old and predictable. This means our rituals and relics are needed more than ever. Children need a place to call home after exploring this ever-changing world.

Our rituals turn the ordinary into the extraordinary. Our Saturdays would have been just chore days without the mystery waffles. Traditions build good memories of quality time, not just passing time and checking lists. This goes beyond mere sentimentality or obsessively detailed repetitions we can never alter. This isn't about resisting change, but seeing the possibilities of growing in place.

We can take time to celebrate in this present moment with the people we love the most. This sends a lifelong message that we not only value our children but we value *us—our family—*as well.

Questions

What are some of your family's rituals?

What is one memory you want to preserve by a photo or a related object?

Is your home tradition rich or poor?

What changes would allow your schedule to be friendlier to regular family gatherings?

What one new simple tradition can you create to add to your week?

Part Three

LAUNCHING INTO LIFE

A large framed photograph stands guard in the hallway by our sons' old rooms. Taken by Mark's sister on a family vacation in Hawaii, it captures Jon and Tim, ages three and five, sipping chilled fresh liquid from brown hairy coconuts. We had stopped at a roadside stand, and they begged to sample this treat. But in the photo, their faces betray their actual experience: this doesn't exactly taste like what we were hoping.

But we were proud of their enthusiastic curiosity. This same wonder would give them courage to sample the rest of life. By adolescence, they were still finding curious coconuts to taste, ideas to explore, and causes to defend. The child with the most coconuts wins.

Watching our babies run out of our homes as young adults is the most exhilarating and yet intimidating part of our parenting story. Our grown children are acquiring a taste for independence, and we are learning to let go.

Chapter 12

RAISING ANALOG KIDS IN A DIGITAL WORLD

The Family beyond Cyberspace

BY MARK

I get the feeling I'm in between
A machine and a man who only looks like me....
Feels like I travel but I never arrive
I wanna thrive not just survive.
—Switchfoot, "Thrive"

In the 2008 Disney-Pixar movie *Wall-E*, the challenge of the digital age is tackled in the form of an animated science-fiction comedy. The yellow robot protagonist, Wall-E, is focused on cleaning up waste-covered Earth and eventually meets his romantic robot counterpart, Eve. Meanwhile, another story is being written in outer space.

The StarLiner *Axiom* is cruising the galaxy with the young human survivors of Earth who are now morbidly obese. Because computers do everything for them on this pampering space cruise ship, they are passive creatures who wait indefinitely to return and repopulate Earth. Before the ultimate computer mutiny by Auto and the GO-4 units, the computers exhibit signs of intelligent life, including volition, greed, and the ability to love, while humans have lost these personal traits. Humans and computers seem to have switched roles.

The movie *Wall-E* ultimately asks whether people will take responsibility for the planet and their own lives or just leave it to the computers. The answer this film hopes we discover is that we can choose our future.

Friend or Foe

The question on the minds of most of us as parents is, how will cyber reality shape my child's life? The TV that changed the world for two generations is now the grandparent of billions of digital media babies. The toys, ranging from laptops, iPods, tablets, and smart-phones, are new vehicles for countless connections and experiences. Are these tech tools friend or foe?

The answer is yes. They are both. Technology has largely been our friend, helping us perform tasks quicker, more accurately, and more consistently. Transportation, science, medicine, education, government, sports, media, and entertainment are all now depen-dent on binary code. The positive effect on society is clear. What is unclear, however, is how this technology reshapes what we know to be human. If unchecked, what happens to our relationships, the family, and particularly the most vulnerable, our children?

Amid shouting from both sides, literature and research abound with the pros and cons of mass media.[1] Those arguing the advantages of technology sound a bit like Auto, the supercomputer in *Wall-E*, assuring us, "You will survive." Those concerned about the negatives sound more like the human captain: "I don't want to survive. I want to live."

This is the ongoing conversation that we want to brave in this chapter. None of us has a clear formula to impose on anyone else; I certainly don't. But I hope to stir all of us to look again at our gadgets and ask, How does a healthy family not just survive but thrive in this web of artificial intelligence? Could the same values that guide my family in other areas also apply to technology?

Values by Which to Live

In the 1980s, Jan and I welcomed our boxy beige personal computer the same way we approached all media—with a cautiously stiff handshake. We were the digital immigrants who could never pose as natives.[2] Our children and grandchildren, however, use technology the way we breathe air.[3]

That early Macintosh and our first flip phone launched us into cyberspace. Here, orbited by an ever-changing swirl of devices, we continue our daily struggle to maintain balance, along with everyone else.

Having an overall philosophy of use has been helpful: Our values can determine our involvement. We believe the same values we applied to the old technology of TV and radios are also relevant to the new. What matters most to us as a family? How then can we use these new tools to serve that end? Focusing on values seems more realistic than setting rules. Rules can be stiffly legalistic, unable to bend as culture changes and our kids age. But our family values can help us flexibly fit new technology into our unique situation and life season.

In our sons' late grade school years, their friends were having sleepovers with VHS entertainment. (I know this sounds archaic, but trust me, it was exciting stuff in the 1980s.) We saw this as an opportunity to also initiate movie nights. We wanted to offer good stories, and included conversations about what we liked or disliked about the scenes, to shape their inner film critics. Leaning into this experience meant sorting through several conflicting values: We prized exposing them to culture but also their innocence, having friends while also holding their own views. On a few occasions, Jon or Tim called to be picked up from a friend's because they didn't want to continue watching a sexually explicit or violent film.

Even though technology has moved well beyond VHS, our values are always relevant. These red and green lights can escort us through the shifting maze of technology so that it remains a positive tool. These qualities also protect our kids' purpose—to grow up fully alive, living beyond the borders of self.

What we value fits under the larger umbrella of being human, safeguarding what is personal because we are, in fact, raising persons, not machines. Because what can potentially take the biggest hit from this mortal-machine dance is our humanity. The danger is not imminently physical, as in the loss of our species. Rather, it is the erosion of our souls. In kid terms, it is threatening childhood.

Realizing that each family will approach all things digital uniquely, here are several values that helped us find our way: keep it real, grow the imagination, stay personal, guard quality time, and protect childhood.

Keep It Real: Active Is Better Than Passive

> *Cypher: You know, I know this steak doesn't exist. I know*
> *that when I put it in my mouth, the Matrix is telling my*
> *brain that it is juicy and delicious. After nine years, you know*
> *what I realize? (Takes a bite of steak.) Ignorance is bliss.*
> —*The Matrix*

I applaud how our expanding world of technology has democratized creative endeavors. A junior high garage band can record their own album and publish their songs to the world, thanks to software and the Internet. An aspiring high school videographer can become instantly famous for his original short clip on YouTube. Media inspires media and is lighting imaginative fires in kids all over the world. From this perspective, technology is a clever, willing servant to young minds.

But like any powerful vehicle, it can jump tracks and cause unintended damage. The danger is that our technological world can encroach on the real. The virtual can be so engaging we don't realize what we are missing in hands-on experiences. When my TV is on, I am drawn away from reading that good book or a conversation with my wife. This is especially true for our children who are just beginning their exploration.

Folks have actually measured this through CT scans and MRIs. The brain of a person who is active in real play scans differently than a brain involved in virtual play. Handling an actual ball activates the frontal cortex and integrates with the whole brain, while a virtual ball arouses the brain without integrating with the whole.[4] Virtual play, although entertaining, is no substitute for physical play in developing the minds of our children.[5]

What attracts us to a Rembrandt canvas is the artist's beautiful response to creation itself. Without the real world, the painting would have no reference point. Too often we are like museum patrons enjoying lovely painted landscapes when we could walk into the countryside for a picnic. Increasingly, we look at life conceptually from the outside instead of enjoying it from the inside. At some point, we want to leave the museum and step into the painting—the real world.

Having this media at my fingertips is like inviting circus clowns to live at my house. They will always steal the show with noisy antics, balloon animals, and nonstop chatter. I need to find ways to lock up these slick virtual entertainers for long stretches, bringing them out only for short bursts when needed. I don't need to be perpetually entertained; I can entertain myself with the real.

I grew up in a neighborhood of boys. During football season, we would watch a televised game impatiently for an hour until, finally, we grabbed a pigskin and shouted, "Let's play!" On the muddy school field across the street, we negotiated plays, got hit, and felt the thrill of crossing the goal line with the football in our grimy hands.

Virtual is entertaining; real is better. Being real involves pain, problems, frustration, perseverance, but also my volition, group consensus, and authentic rewards. Engaging in the real moves my whole self from being a passive spectator to courageously running onto the field of life.

Grow the Imagination: Unstructured Is Better Than Structured

Play is the highest form of research.
—Albert Einstein

If you want to be creative, stay in part a child, with the creativity and invention that characterizes children before they are deformed by adult society.
—Jean Piaget

We had witnessed our kids become zombielike after watching an inconsequential TV show. Media is mesmerizing, a bright, pulsating light to a child's open mind. We also noticed that after too much of this artificial stimulation, their self-initiative and creativity were gone, like a sugar low after candy.

Our biggest concern with media, both the TV and tech tools, was to protect our young sons' sprouting imaginations. Real experiences cause children to pivot around their own thoughts, while the virtual confines them to someone else's ideas. Compounding the problem, too much media makes our children passive.[6] Couch potatoes come to mind.

The same family that gave us their old black-and-white TV also gifted our kids with an Atari video game system. They were the media Santas for our deprived children. Our first computer game, Pac-Man, had that same hypnotic power, only perhaps more so because it was interactive. Children love patterns in sight and sound, but the animated, round, hungry creatures met this need in an almost addictive cycle, where the children must play again and again. The Atari joined the black-and-white TV in our basement.

/// **ALL CHILDREN HAVE THE CAPACITY TO IMAGINE, BUT WHEN CAPTIVATING MEDIA IMAGINES FOR THEM, THEIR OWN DREAMS GROW DULL.** /// This loss of imagination is now, a generation later, an enormous concern. Sobering evidence clearly shows that technology can erode our children's imaginative abilities. Ed Miller, of the Alliance for Childhood said, "We're engaged in a huge experiment where we've fundamentally changed the experience of childhood.... We don't know what the outcome is going to be. We're robbing kids of their birthright: the access to free, unstructured play of their own making."[7]

Why is a child's imagination so important? Like discovering fire or inventing the wheel, human imagination protects and expands our quality of life. Everyone's future depends on it. Even the catastrophe of 9/11 was described a "failure of imagination" because that event was not anticipated, despite the warnings.[8] To the graduating class of Stanford University in 2007, poet Dana Gioia declared, "Adult life begins in a child's imagination.... And we've relinquished that imagination to the marketplace."[9] A child's imagination is perhaps the most powerful resource in the world.

Jan and I often found ourselves swimming upstream in consumerist culture to preserve this creative spark. We wanted our sons to be tech savvy but equally recoiled from chasing after the latest game box hitting the shelves. How could we keep them socially and culturally relevant without allowing them to be programmed by intense commercial pressures?

We could continue that open garden landscape of their early childhood, where discovery and choice still fueled curiosity. Once again, we found that less is more—and that boredom can be the imagination's best friend. Of course, like every parent, we heard the words "There's nothing to do" as a personal failure to provide for our kids. But with some encouragement, "You can make something interesting happen," they usually imagined their way out of stagnation. One dull afternoon, stuck at home, Jon designed an indoor miniature golf course. Tim often made games out of paper handouts at boring adult meetings. I wonder how many inventions have been inspired by having nothing better to do?

It's easy to assume that imagination comes with the child package and that it naturally grows with age, like feet or limbs. Sadly, while IQ scores have risen among elementary children, creative scores have significantly decreased, especially among kindergartners through third graders.[10] Many of us never think about protecting creativity. Now we know: The imagination doesn't naturally expand and mature. It needs care and feeding in an uncluttered environment.

Jan and I realized that the best way to grow our kids' imagination was through unstructured play where original ideas could surface through free choice. When Jon and Tim were left alone with a pile of blocks or sand, they needed to size up their options and resources. Their imaginations transported them from boredom to solving problems.

Children take complicated internal steps to use these imaginative muscles: observation, vision, volition, discipline, evaluation, and perseverance. In group play, they develop interpersonal skills to get playmates on board: "You be the captain, and I'll be the pirate." "Let's pretend we are spies." "Want to find the biggest shells and build a sand castle?" As educator Maria Montessori believed, play is the "work" of the child.[11]

We encouraged our kids to get outdoors as much as possible. "When kids are outside playing in an unstructured way, something magical happens," said Molly Ames Baker, advisory committee member of Getting Kids Outdoors. "You can watch it unfold: as all their senses become engaged, they become more curious, creative, inventive. They are experiencing the world on their own terms."[12] Nature is God's gift to our children's imaginations.

Of course, we realized the importance of a nutritious diet, medical checkups, and a safe home. But studies show that promoting our children's imaginations is just as vital to their well-being. That's why the American Academy of Pediatrics recommends keeping children under the age of two as screen-free as possible.[13] Beyond this, Dr. Kenneth Ginsburg of the American Academy of Pediatrics suggested parents set clear guidelines to encourage free play because it is essential to the cognitive, physical, social, and emotional health of children and teens. From a medical perspective, open-ended play is as necessary as eating vegetables and getting enough sleep.[14]

We can't entirely blame technology for our kids' shrinking playtime. Ginsburg also warned that play is being reduced by hurried lifestyles, changes in family structure, academic pressure, unsafe neighborhoods, even organized sports, which can take away our children's freedom to choose.[15] In this brave new world of restricted play, we are off the map in knowing how children will ultimately develop.

Jan's and my instincts told us to limit media and encourage free time in our home. Video games were confined to the weekend, only for one hour and always with a friend. We encouraged research and homework done on the computer, recognizing it as a powerful tool. But the outdoors was our regular habitat. Having a taste for the real, the artificial was not as satisfying. Our children thrived on play that was unstructured by adults, teachers, or computers. As they grew older, they wisely restricted themselves.

Our children will never have wonderful memories of hours spent on video games. They will remember when Tim found some discarded wood and built his own Tom Sawyer's raft with a friend that barely floated, then sank into the nearby backwaters. Jon might recall designing a room-sized marble racetrack with blocks. They will remember climbing a tree simply because it was there to climb or digging a hidden snow fort or writing songs and starting their own band.

In protecting real play for the sake of imagination, we are protecting something even more precious: the creative genius of the Imago Dei. We are God's creative reflections. The God who imaginatively said "Let there be … and there was" encourages us to imperfectly follow as children who dare to imagine what can be.

Stay Personal: Human Is Better Than Human-Made

Several times, I have witnessed well-dressed couples romantically sitting next to each other at an elegant restaurant, each holding not hands but a smartphone, perusing the web or checking for messages.

Jan and I have been that couple. When we have the choice between a live intelligent human next to us or a smart gadget, we want to choose the human.

People matter more than machines. I want this reflected in the simple preference I give to present company, like silencing an indiscriminate phone. I must find ways to humanize my use of technology.

Computers are precise, cheaper to use and maintain, and they don't arrive with moods or interpersonal problems. Understandably, factories around the globe replace people with machinery. Still, if a robot appeared with the elegant complexity of a human being, orders for that digital marvel would flood in. Humans are irreplaceable.

It is easy to forget this lesson in history. The industrial era of the 1800s improved the quality of life in many ways. But those earlier generations also fought hard for the dignity of people trampled by the revolution, establishing laws regarding labor hours, safety regulations, and fair pay. It seems the battle must be fought again.

Certainly, digital tools have enhanced our humanity. Last week, I used FaceTime to say good-bye to my aunt while three thousand miles away before she passed. I can also say hello to my sons halfway around the globe, be reunited with high school buddies, or find my wife in a crowded mall. Through instant photos, I can invite folks not present to share the splendor of a hike or even what I'm about to eat. I feel as if I've just begun to mine these humane benefits.

Still, I know an image is no replacement for a human made in God's image. There are social backlashes to frequenting cyberspace. The ease of communicating produces more than I can humanly handle, and the sheer quantity reduces the quality of my connections.

When I mass market my personal information, how personal is it really? Can a new post replace taking a walk with a friend?

Older kids share this disconnect. Many teens report that although this media has brought them social capital, helped them feel less ostracized,[16] and even caused higher empathy scores,[17] they now have fewer in-depth relationships. They may have more acquaintances, but they are less intimate.[18] Studies have also shown that greater use of the Internet is associated with declines in a teenager's sense of well-being, a lower self-esteem,[19] and weaker social ties.[20] And as the movie *Wall-E* sadly predicts, there is a direct link between obesity among children and increased media use.[21]

Our human capacity to bleed, laugh, choose, remember, taste, feel, desire justice, and believe is beyond any Intel chip. As C. S. Lewis so aptly put it, "There are no *ordinary* people. You have never talked to a mere mortal.... Next to the Blessed Sacrament itself, your neighbor is the holiest object presented to your senses."[22] Obviously, time alone with our computers can't compare with one-on-one people time.

Jan and I fought hard against the temptation of a digital babysitter. It's initially simpler to place our children in front of media to keep them quiet for a while. And of course, there are times of war when we really have no other option but to use the digital toy: to help a wiggly child sit still while you talk to the doctor or while you're on a cross-country flight or enjoying a meal out with friends.

When our sons were tiny, Jan caught a debilitating flu while I was in England. As she lay in bed, she grew suspicious of the silence and crawled downstairs to find them on chairs, pulled up to an open freezer, Popsicles in hand. She could have used a digital tablet that week.

But it can easily become routine to immobilize kids with this quick fix. And the scariest thought is that I am modeling what it means to be human and my own interface with technology will be cloned. Would I be surprised if a robot companion walked through my front door instead of my child, asking whether it would suffice for the evening? I sadly see our folks and their senior friends fixated on their big-screen TVs. Having a family meal or hearing about the day from a digital agent is not a close second to our own flesh and blood. When I am older, I will long for those little human faces.

I want to rule over machines, rather than let them be my dictators. I am daily fighting this battle to move people to the front, ahead of technology, to have uninterrupted meals, have cyber-free nights, and go to bed at the same time as my spouse does, not staying up answering email. And when I must be on the computer, I don't have to be isolated.

We had our family computer centrally located. Now we all carry little computers in our pockets, and I appreciate the access to time-sensitive messages. But do I need to check my smartphone every time it sends an alert? Only a small percentage of the time do I find a text with an actual emergency, so I wonder, what am I missing? Curiosity is a quality that gets exploited by my devices. I want to hold sacred the gift of the present company. I want to pay attention to people.

I think our expanding social media points to our need for authentic relationships in a functional, digital world. Having coffee with a friend is more satisfying than corresponding with almost friends on social media. The digital café phenomenon is a perfect case in point, where dozens of folks peck away on their devices.

They are working together separately. They would rather float in that pool of strangers than work at home alone.

Recently, Pope Francis described the Internet as "a gift from God." But he continued, "Maybe many young people waste too many hours on futile things ... chatting on the Internet or with smartphones, watching TV ... and [using] the products of techno-logical progress, which should simplify and improve the quality of life, but distract attention away from what is really important." He cautioned that our digital world must become "a network not of wires but of people."[23] Well said. Being wired will never replace being well connected to another human.

Guard Quality Time: Present Is Better Than Distracted

My consumption of media is like eating potato chips: I can never enjoy just one. And like the empty calories of fried starch, my time is often wasted. In the hindsight of several decades, I deeply regret the time lost zoning out on meaningless content. But our children, from tiny to teens, live with the youthful myth of immortality, not understanding that each minute spent is irretrievable.

At first glance, media is certainly a time saver. Perhaps the reason time seems to be moving faster is that *we* are moving faster, thanks to our digital servants. But I often wonder, in the self-checkout or when ordering a book online or when paying bills via a recording, where have all the people gone? Efficiency is not always personal.

Actually, our digital lifestyle both saves time and squanders time. A 2010 study found that children and teens spend an average of seven hours and fifty-eight minutes on entertainment media each day. That is almost fifty-six hours a week, up more than seven hours a week from the same study in 2004.[24] That's one-third of their year not being present.

And the cost may be more than time. Studies show that children who have limitless access to online activities are more prone to mental health problems such as depression. Students who flip back and forth from studying to social media had worse grades. Those who spent more hours on media experienced more sick days and poorer behavior in school. There is an alarming correlation between social media and signs of many mental disorders, including narcissism, antisocial personality, bipolar disorder, and borderline personality disorder.[25] The bottom line: humans need quality time with one another to stay sane.

More alarming, research shows that some excessive tech consumers exhibit addictive behavior. Experts fall short of calling it an addiction, but many users have all the classic symptoms. The treatment for this behavior is also the same.[26] A bigger question is, what is everyone avoiding? Is this just a distraction from pain? Often the secrecy and aloneness of the digital world give it more power. But when we mask loneliness through a device, it only deepens the problem. One likely theory is that as parents become more attached to technology, they become detached from their kids, who in turn attach themselves to their devices.[27] This is a warning for all ages simply to unplug.

Yes, people take time, while machines appear to save it. But there may be a high price: the loss of authentic relationships, which require quality time. We no longer know the grocer's first name or the bookseller's favorite author. By reducing life to ones and zeros, we have removed the intricate complexity of human interaction. Unlike jaguars that roam in solitude, people are social creatures. If this defining feature is altered, what will the next generation of humans be like? Saying time is valuable is not the same as saying time is money. Often the two are at war.

Only clear boundaries and disciplined restraint can protect our precious quality time. Each device needs its own leash to make it subservient to us. Just three out of ten kids say their parents set and maintain limits on their media use, according to a Kaiser Family Foundation study.[28] I'm guessing it's because we adults also struggle to rein in our usage. I don't need to watch every movie or download every song or send every picture on Instagram. I must remember these machines are merely tools that extend from human hands. I can master my tech toys to submit to my twenty-four-hour limits.

Stuart and Jill Briscoe ask their visiting grandchildren to place their smartphones in a basket at the door.[29] The point: if you've come to visit us, why are you texting someone else? Our undivided attention expresses value to another.

When some of my friends meet for lunch, they place their phones in the center of the table. Whoever first answers his or her phone pays the bill. One family we know practices regular media fasts. Another family owns just one flip phone to be used for emergencies only by whoever is away from home.

Each family must continually wrestle with how to harness the good of their devices without compromising their core values. It begins with accepting our mortal limitations of time and space. In our attempts to be omnipresent and omniscient, we can miss the greatest gift of all: this present moment. Dividing our time can create a hierarchy in which the current company ranks beneath the physically absent who have our digital presence. Relationships thrive on focused attention, not multitasking.

Performing musicians sometimes de-clutter a stage from the busyness of too many instruments so they can hear their voices. Less is more, in music and in life. Quality time, intentionally guarded, allows us to hear the voices we love the most.

Protect Childhood: Goodness and Innocence Are Priceless Gifts

We left town for a week, accidentally leaving our garage door wide open, visible from the street. Thankfully, we were not robbed and the only intruders were dead leaves. Maybe the burglars figured no one who possessed valuables would leave their home so unguarded.

The Internet is a wide-open portal that makes our home vulnerable to anyone's indiscriminate actions, opinions, or vulgarity. As parents, Jan and I wanted to closely monitor all incoming content, knowing that our children's impressionable minds were at stake.

In our Western world, we often process thoughts in a linear pattern. We think in terms of cause and effect, action and reaction. But real life is complex, more like an agricultural model where we reap what we sow. Our actions are circular, and my choices loop back to affect me. This then becomes a new cause, creating a new effect. I don't simply act on my laptop, giving it one-way commands. It also acts on me. Children are especially porous, so that whatever touches each sense leaves an indelible mark within.

We often treat our minds as neutral free agents or blank slates. But our brains are easily biased by repeated experiences and thoughts. The brain's plasticity allows us to create mental pathways that become familiar. We can create thought habits that become louder than our original voices.

Studies show that media violence makes all people, including kids, more aggressive. Similarly, exposure to sexually explicit material can lead to distorted views and greater sexual preoccupation.[30] In another tragic loss of innocence, the harmful effects of cyberbullying are well documented, causing loneliness, stress, depression, aggression, and even suicidal thoughts.[31]

/// CHILDREN ARE UNBAKED COOKIE DOUGH. AS PARENTS, WE HAVE THE WEIGHTY RESPONSIBILITY OF DETERMINING WHO AND WHAT IS SHAPING THEM. /// A sad consequence of the garden rebellion in Genesis 3 was the loss of innocence. We can still see this simple trust flickering in the eyes of the very young. The root meaning of the word *innocence* is "harmless; not noxious." Recognizing media's potential to poison our young is very sobering. Since we may not completely know the fallout from skipping over the innocent years, Jan and I were committed to enjoying the benefits of technology without allowing it to raise our kids too quickly.

Create Momentum

In drivers training, I was taught not to brake during a turn. I learned to slow down before the turn, then accelerate out of it. Hitting the brakes on a curve could cause a dangerous skid and loss of control. As parents, we are often surprised by the curves, then react by riding the brakes in white-knuckle fear. But when we lose momentum, we lose control of the direction our kids are heading. If at all possible, we must find a way to accelerate through this digital turn.

The industrial revolution also thrust a new situation on children and parents. Our society intervened with child labor laws and other necessary protections. Cultural values protected the nuclear family. Next, radio and TV generations had to establish value-based guidelines to protect young audiences. Now our digital generation must do the same. We must anticipate the curves and apply appropriate brakes, or the most vulnerable will be hurt on this potentially dangerous curve.

The trick with toddlers (and me, for that matter) is to find a better option when taking something away. Simply saying no is not a happy approach. We all respond best with the acceleration of an exciting substitution rather than a dead-end denial.

One afternoon, I found Jon engrossed in a game of Marble Madness on our G3 computer. Before I could react with "Time to quit," I noticed he had beaten my best score. The competitor overrode the responsible referee, as we both hunched over the keyboard for the next hour. This became our new normal for that medium: we would do it together.

Acceleration requires input from everyone. A starting place might be a reality check, to keep a log of everyone's Internet use for three days.[32] We also need to have calm conversations about what need is driving both parents and kids to spend hours on social media, digital games, or just perusing the endless Internet. Instead of FaceTime, we can create face-to-face opportunities, incentives for friends to come over with physical games or even technology that is more challenging, creative, and sociable. We can push the accelerator down to give everyone a fresh direction.

We play a game with our grandkids called Silly Siri Stories. We pass the phone around quickly to record our voices making up a wild tale. Then we play back the transcript, laughing hysterically at all the misinterpretations. Our grandson also uses the phone to create original movies. I've enjoyed watching my granddaughters perform impromptu shows with the help of wireless speakers and a digital song bank.

As a parent, I see myself as a coach; I can't stay on defense. I want to move the ball with my offensive squad on the field. When I push back with a defensive no, I must follow through quickly with a brilliant offense. /// A YES TO SOMETHING GOOD IS ALWAYS MORE POWERFUL THAN A NO TO SOMETHING BAD. ///

We can creatively brainstorm with our children to find the yes. Our two sons joined swim, soccer, and surf teams; learned tennis and rock climbing; built models; learned magic tricks; wrote plays; and read good books. They spent hours with friends at the beach. We tried to follow our sons' passions to find their true norths rather than imposing our map. Our hope was that by early adolescence, we had nourished their natural gifts enough so they could create their own momentum.

This inner drive will help our kids steer their own courses in the rapids of technology. An encouragement to parents who find themselves drowning in white water: there is still time to help your child dig deep to find his or her yes.

Analog Kids

As long as we've been a family, we've used record players. A basic one now sits on a shelf in the center of our house, with an assortment of old and new records below. We have iPods and CD players and use music apps with quality speakers in most rooms. But still, we like the romance of picking out a familiar cardboard jacket, pulling the record from the dust cover, handling it from only the edges, and placing it carefully on the spindle of the turntable. Then we flip a simple switch, watch the player spin, and set the needled arm down gently and precisely onto the black vinyl. After a bit of soft crackle, like magic, the music begins. Children especially love to watch and wonder how a spinning black circle could create those sounds.

This is an analog musical experience, where the sound waves are analogous to the original instruments and voices. There is a direct connection to the sound source, which reproduces the original pulsating air into an electrical signal. The record player needle then translates this signal as music to our ears. It can utilize the full range of sound waves because the substance determines the form or waves. Some would describe analog as more authentic, having a warmer tone.

Digital sounds are produced differently. They take the original sound and reconstruct it with a limited set of numbers. It makes a convincing copy, easily mass-produced, uniform, and accessible with one touch and a few seconds' time. Its sounds can also be tweaked on either end of recording, so you may never know what the original was like. The reproduced sound waves are limited by the sets of numbers, so the form dictates the substance.

We tried our best to raise analog kids who were connected directly to the source, whether it was handling the fish they just caught or learning about lightning after a storm or having their own friendships with God. Although this isn't always easy or realistic, we wanted to take our kids back to the origins of things so they could appreciate the beautiful complexity of life. Eating a store-bought orange is not the same as picking one off the tree you planted from a seed when you were five. Having this kind of experiential knowledge gives kids ownership. It grows wisdom in an age of information.

Most important, we wanted to *be* the real thing, with real struggles and real laughter or tears, and move beyond performance to the unpredictable dynamic of authentic relationships.

The world is actually analog, as our culture is increasingly digital. But we believe the ease of pushing a button cannot replace the reward of the painstaking, cumbersome effort required of learning something firsthand, especially growing relationships. We don't want to settle for kids who just imitate sound bites from a popular source. We want our kids to be authentic, primary sources of substantive life for others.

Questions

Would you describe your use of technology as controlled, out of control, or somewhere in between? What practical limits can you set in place for your own life?

In taking a realistic look at your children's use of technology, how many hours per day or week are they in front of a screen?

What practical limitations do you want to set on this usage?

What fresh momentum can you encourage to unplug yourself and your family?

Chapter 13

THE DISCERNING CONSUMER

Questioning the System

BY JAN

Face this world. Learn its ways, watch it, be careful of too hasty guesses at its meaning. In the end you will find clues to it all.
—H. G. Wells, *The Time Machine*

I wasn't always a skeptic regarding cultural norms. I ran with the herd in junior high, wearing my brand-name flats and short skirts, attending the right parties, and only sitting by certain people in the cafeteria.

My cultural skepticism began with the birth of our first son, Jon. I had barely caught a glimpse of his gorgeous pink face, crowned with golden hair, when he was whisked away to be cleaned and brought to me *hours* later, after I arrived in my hospital room. Then, I was allowed to hold him for only twenty short minutes before he was again shuttled away with the other infants on the floor. This impersonal routine was that medical institution's old-fashioned way to deliver multiple newborns to a dorm full of mommies: Only a quick visit allowed every few hours. No time for bonding—too impractical.

And I wondered, *This may be their normal, but is it best for me and my child?* And my questioning has never stopped.

In the wild, running with the herd is often nature's method of protection for its vulnerable young. But the human herd is not necessarily running where we want to go, especially with our children. As we anticipate the launching years, as early as ten through perhaps twenty, we need to know our cultural terrain.

When our sons were adolescents, a favorite activity was four wheeling in a used Land Cruiser we named the Silver Hind. Late one afternoon, we were exploring the stark beauty of Joshua Tree National Park and realized it was almost dark. Glancing casually at our map, we spotted a dirt road that looked well traveled and headed back in the direction of the freeway for our drive home. To our nervous surprise, the road gradually got rougher until, miles later, it became a narrow creek bed, with boulders the size of crates. Now the sun was down, and the gas tank near empty. Thankfully, we finally managed to reach civilization.

That haphazard family ride is not how we want to approach the sometimes friendly, also threatening culture with kids. We cannot assume that the familiar roads, even the well-traveled ones, will get us home. We are surrounded by creative human endeavors from centuries of intelligent, caring humans. Our journey demands constant due diligence to stay on top of this ever-shifting topography. It also requires great courage to find a different road, even carving our own if necessary.

We want to grow kids who are actively engaging in culture, not just passively influenced by it. Here is a delicate balance: If we step back and allow our children to drink freely from the cultural fire hose, they will become saturated to the point of absorption. But if we completely flee civilization, as Jonah did, we are abandoning our children's purpose to be the image of God on earth.

From earliest civilizations, culture has connected individuals in a common bond. Whether in dress or feasts, or rites of passage, every culture is a complex collection of creative expression, beliefs, and behaviors endorsed by the majority of folks. Like strong, invisible threads, these acceptable ways of thinking and behaving also pull hard on families. This is why we care about culture; it's human glue. We care about our culture because we care about people and what shapes their lives.

No culture on earth is completely evil or benign. We have to pick and choose. The off-the-grid survivalists or religious escapists do not change their world by withdrawing. Only perceptive consumers can alter the cultural landscape. For our children to make a significant dent, we must risk entering this sphere with not only confidence but also alert discernment. To open our children's eyes, we believed we needed to fortify them in several areas:

- Build an awareness of history to develop objectivity
- Expose them to the common good to develop a timeless taste

- Introduce them to various global cultures to see differences
- Talk about current events to foster analytical thinking
- Take them to the edge to discover their purpose

Humbly Learning from the Past

My original title for this book was *How to Raise a Dinosaur*. This was inspired by C. S. Lewis's referring to himself as a dinosaur in his inaugural Cambridge lecture. In claiming to be a representative of an older era, Lewis acknowledged the reluctance of moderns to look back on history, stating that we "don't want to be lectured on Neanderthal Man by a Neanderthal, still less on dinosaurs by a dinosaur." But he went on to argue, "If a live dinosaur dragged its slow length into the laboratory, would we not all look back as we fled? What a chance to know at last how it really moved and looked and smelled and what noises it made!" Lewis then presented himself to Cambridge as that dinosaur, saying, "Use your specimen while you can. There are not going to be many more dinosaurs."[1]

Young dinosaurs can still be found. These are children who not only have the limited vision of conventional trends, dressing like a superhero or finding the latest toy in a Happy Meal, but they also have traveled back in time. By imagining earlier civilizations, they gain a depth that can more easily navigate current culture. Children who have this humble willingness to learn from the past are becoming extremely rare. Like an endangered species, they are threatened by their environment, which ironically applauds conformity to the latest innovation.

As a lover of medieval literature, C. S. Lewis was also facing extinction as he lived under the edict of "Our modern perception is the truest and best."[2] Yet he was the consummate model for the interface of Christians and culture. At one point, he was the second most influential person in Britain, behind Churchill. This dinosaur left some enormous footprints.

Lewis influenced his world from the perspective of time. He dared to write, "The only palliative is to keep the clean sea breeze of the centuries blowing through our minds, and this can be done only by reading old books."[3] My translation: we need the past to inform the present. /// **IF CHILDREN RECEIVE INPUT ONLY FROM MASS MEDIA, THEY WILL GET LOST IN THE JUNGLE OF NOW.** ///

Our breeze from past centuries came from several directions. We savored classics from the library, as well as great modern stories. Of course, we had our pets: Lewis and Tolkien. We also visited (sometimes dragged our kids to) near and out-of-the-way historical sites, retelling the fascinating true stories. We watched them act out plays based on those characters.

Museums were also an easy way to go back in time. Our sons were inspired to copy Egyptian hieroglyphics, build models of famous planes, and create their own inventions by seeing contraptions from antiquity. Listening to my dad's World War II tales of being shot out of the sky as a B-24 pilot, then surviving a German POW camp gave them a point of reference for defeat in a soccer game.

We included classical music in our family sound track and talked about music's colorful characters and history. We bought inexpensive musical instruments: a kazoo, recorder, mouth harp, and gourd shakers. We have a growing collection of unusual instruments from other cultures.

In the tale *Beowulf,* "an old sword is expected to be better than a new one." In our progressive world, each generation is tempted to believe it invented truth. But wisdom humbly stands on the shoulders of people who have already lived well. For our children to be articulate writers of modern history, they must learn the stories of past generations.

Developing a Timeless Taste

I wish we could have taken our young sons to Europe. Our closest encounter with centuries-old architecture was in Washington, DC. We were awestruck standing under the elaborate Capitol dome and strolling the vast, precisely laid paths on the mall, centered on the impressive Washington Monument.

Visiting DC was part of our grand scheme: We wanted to spread out a banquet of quality cultural choices for our kids. Like knowing human history, sampling art from past generations can create a more discerning taste in a drive-through culture. Just as eating a good diet gives an appreciation for healthy food, we hoped to inspire an appetite for enduring goodness—a timeless taste.

One summer night, we sat on the lawn opposite the Charles River listening to the Boston Pops orchestra. This dynamic musical experience introduced our kids to the world of symphony, falling asleep to Tchaikovsky. We also took in local free concerts and watched friends perform in our living room or at neighborhood coffee bars. We listened to current hits and dissected the lyrics.

We stopped to watch amateur outdoor artists and stared at paintings by Monet, Picasso, and Van Gogh, glad to live in the same general neighborhood. We took them to kid-friendly ballets and dramas, and library puppet shows. And I already mentioned reading great literature.

Our postmodern world throws all art under a subjective bus: "What is good, beautiful, and true to you may not be to me." This prevailing philosophy in our culture has contextualized *everything* to be good, beautiful, and true only in that individualized context. Sometimes believers are insecure about hazarding a critique or entering this marketplace of ideas about cultural goods. But goodness is not relative: Helping a stranger find an address, seeing your infant's first smile, giving an honest compliment, and making a quality product are all no doubt good. We believe timeless truth, beauty, and goodness are self-evident. Like wood floating to the surface, it always emerges no matter how far a society pushes it down.

In *The Evidential Power of Beauty*, Thomas Dubay argued that beauty is not simply arbitrary or subjective, but humans know beauty when they see it.[4] Even a trip to a national park or the seashore will help build our kids' taste for beauty. On their own they can discern and appreciate the lasting artistry of the real from plastic, veneer, or synthetic glamour.

We wanted our young children exposed to a wide variety of the common good, to enjoy the best achievements of culture, whether it was a Bach cantata or John Coltrane. Mark often listened to Jon and Tim's favorite Beatles or Led Zeppelin tunes, exploring with them the musical genius and meaning of the words. In our sampling of creativity, we encouraged thinking out loud. Rather than taking a right-versus-wrong approach, we appreciated all works on a scale of bad, okay, and good, better, best. That kept our conversations alive and honest, encouraging their own discovery.

This exploration not only includes the world of arts but also the world of ideas. When one son was a first-semester freshman in college, he called Mark, disturbed about his philosophy class. A lecture on religion had rocked his world. So Mark drove down to walk the campus, listening and responding to his thoughts for two hours. In the end, Mark agreed with the university professor: God could not be absolutely proved rationally, nor could unbelief. But then Mark added, "I don't want to believe in a god who could be written down on a piece of paper, folded up, and pulled out of my pocket for proof. All are beliefs, and even atheism or consumerism is built on faith."

This encouraged our son to be fearless and tenacious in his pursuit of truth. All truth is God's truth. Not all truth is eternally saving, but all truth belongs to God. We wanted our kids to know they should never back away from what might be discovered.

The Transforming Power of Travel

The whole object of travel is not to set foot on foreign land; it is at last to set foot on one's own country as a foreign land.
—G. K. Chesterton, "The Riddle of the Ivy"

Beyond time travel through history and art, actual travel can dramatically change our children's perspectives. From an unfamiliar place, they'll have a new vantage point from which to view their known world. We regret that we didn't travel more with our young children.

But our relocations, from the West to the East Coast, then down to the southern United States, definitely broadened our kids' worldview.

Jon was privileged to join other adolescent leaders in Australia and New Zealand, and Tim traveled as a young ambassador to view the unfamiliar political world of DC, which was mind expanding for both. We also took numerous surf trips to Mexico, where we practiced our Spanish, snagged roadside fish tacos, and searched for waves. Otherwise, the most stretching moments were when we simply encountered people who challenged our comfort zones.

/// **VISITING DIFFERENT CULTURES CREATES A GOOD DISEQUILIBRIUM.** /// We realize there are other ways to dress or spend free time with no electricity or communicate without words. We notice the simple pleasure of picking a ripe mango and the easy joy of kids who have very little.

From the beginning of time, God has loved the whole world. The apostle Paul demonstrated this in the book of Acts as he stood in front of the Areopagus on Mars Hill, far from his hometown. There amid the intellectuals of Athens, Paul brought two worlds together as monotheism met pantheism. Rather than confronting these philosophers, he moved onto their turf, finding commonality. Seeing an unknown-god statue, he assumed God had arrived before he had. Paul knew God was actively at work in all cultures (Acts 17:23).

Christianity is neither Western nor Eastern, but transforms all civilizations. We can unconsciously wed Christianity and our culture into a petrified state of unholy matrimony. In this self-centered worldview, we lose perspective on what is eternal truth and what is just our temporal setting. Traveling to other places can cure this tendency and give us a fresh look at our own homeostasis.

This may be the greatest bonus for all our kids: Each new setting exposes them to the vastness of God's love. Rather than being threatened, God just gets bigger.

Analyze This: Current Events

Almost everything in our national culture, even the news, has
been reduced to entertainment, or altogether eliminated.
—Dana Gioia

Travel lets your children stand on the global stage. No longer statistics, children who lack school supplies now have names and faces. Maybe our kids witnessed how corrupt law enforcement makes everyday life unsafe for innocent folks. Faraway places are identifiable on a map. What happens halfway around the world now affects our home.

Even if we never leave American soil, we can read and discuss important issues with our kids, including history in the making: Why do you think all the refugees are fleeing that country? Did you know that one in six people in our country struggle with hunger? What do you think about half of the kids your age spending more than forty hours a week in front of a screen? How well do you think that politician communicated? What do you think our state should do about the drought? If you could, would you buy an electric car? How has the relationship between our two countries changed since that leader took power?

Ignorance is not bliss. In a recent poll of one thousand adults conducted by the American Revolution Center, more Americans identified Michael Jackson as the composer of "Beat It" than knew the Bill of Rights was part of the Constitution. Also alarming, 29 percent couldn't name the current vice president and over 80 percent were unable to name a single Supreme Court justice.[5] But what is more concerning is the apparent lack of curiosity about the people and ideas that govern our lives. And if these are the adults, we can't expect the kids to care either.

When we talk about our political system or the international community, we are educating our kids for their future. If we love our children, we'll make sure they are paying attention.

Take Kids to the Edge of Themselves

Believing takes practice.

—Madeleine L'Engle, *A Wind in the Door*

Mark and I are often asked how to best reinforce a teenager's faith in God. The answer, we believe, is to take teens to an uncomfortable place where these young or almost believers must wrestle with their convictions in a climate of real need. Serve meals to the homeless, adopt a military family, help build a house in Mexico, befriend a lonely senior at a nursing facility, or visit a slum in India, an orphanage in Kathmandu, or a dump in Nicaragua. This will put the teenagers' faith on the line and allow them to realize the importance of believing. At the edge of their own resources, young people see firsthand why knowing God matters.

Without this intentional push, it's like trying to balance a bike without peddling. When faith gets separated from this momentum of tangible giving, we are just being nice Christians, trying to behave but largely irrelevant to society. We live in a dynamic, entertaining world, so having personal devotions and attending church can seem meaningless—or just boring. Faith is simply one more self-focused exercise: trying to be good. But what are we good *for*? At the edge, our kids can connect their spiritual practices to practical needs. We are not simply preserving their faith. We are strengthening our young to discover their ultimate purpose: to enter culture with realistic belief that transforms.

Adolescents have a sense of destiny as they approach that mysterious land of adulthood. They want their lives to matter, to leave deep footprints. The poet Muriel Strode famously wrote, "I will not follow where the path may lead, but I will go where there is no path, and I will leave a trail."[6] Young people intuitively believe they can do this. We can show them they don't have to wait to make a difference.

You Go Out There with Those Biting Flies: Real and Perceived Dangers

It was so muggy our eyelids were sweating. We were on an August surf trip in Cape Hatteras with another all-boy family. An hour earlier, we had dragged our bodies, towels, beach umbrellas, and surfboards up the dunes to our vacation rental. Immense thunderclouds and gusty winds were threatening our late afternoon fun. Now we sat motionless in the dark beach house, almost grateful for the power outage that kept us still.

We traded stories from the day about waves ridden and how many green-head fly or mosquito bites we could count. Every few minutes, the whole room was illuminated by a blinding burst of lightning.

Suddenly, one of us remembered we had left towels out on the clothesline, and it was starting to pour rain. Who wanted to grab them quick?

"You go out there with those biting flies," our youngest member yelled. And we all burst into incredulous laughter: his fear of being struck by lightning paled next to his dread of another insect bite.

That expression became our household cliché for unreal, imagined dangers. As we prepare our kids to enter a culture that is not entirely safe, it's very important that we, as parents, sort through our own exaggerated anxieties. An overreaction to fear can erupt into something far worse.

Parents who overprotect now have a name: helicopter parents. This came from teens who complained about hovering adults.[7] This overparenting can happen when we fear negative consequences, which we believe could be avoided if we intervened. These aren't life-threatening dangers, just uncomfortable, less-than-perfect possibilities. Biting flies.

/// THE GREATEST GIFT WE CAN GIVE OUR CHILDREN AS THEY FACE INDEPENDENCE IS TRANSFERRED RESPONSIBILITY FOR THEIR OWN LIVES. /// When we continually second-guess their choices or shield them from hard lessons—completing their homework, filling out job applications, disallowing a wide swath of cultural experiences—we sabotage their own abilities to make good decisions later in life. And that lightning strike is an actual danger.

Another biting fly is a fear of failure, either for our children or for us. We hesitate to enroll them in dance class because they might not like it; we avoid baseball sign-ups in case they just sit on the bench; we won't attempt that building project together because we've never been good with our hands. Sometimes we are the child's greatest inhibition and reason for inertia. We both need to take risks. As G. K. Chesterton aptly put it, "If a thing is worth doing, it is worth doing badly."[8]

On the other hand, I've known parents who were in denial about very real and present dangers. One sultry Virginia afternoon, our son and his friend decided to paddle across the wide Lynnhaven River channel, a distance of about one-third mile. The warm waters were thick with jellyfish, but the greater, undetected threat was an approaching thunderhead. After hearing the first boom of thunder, we watched helplessly from shore as their two small forms furiously paddled surfboards against the strong wind and a black backdrop that crackled with lightning.

Why hadn't we paid more attention to their conversation at lunch when this plan had been conceived? Of course, we had thunderstorms most summer afternoons, but we could only imagine a fun, safe adventure, not this near tragedy. Thankfully, prayers were answered and they lived to tell the story.

We want to believe the best about our kids. We can't imagine the actual dangers because we don't want to. But if we ignore the subtle alarms of increasing moodiness or disinterest in activities, or if we avoid difficult conversations about unhealthy friendships, our denial can only increase any pending danger.

Another unnoticed danger in our culture might be "nature-deficit disorder," named by Richard Louv in his book *Last Child in the Woods*. He attributed children's increased depression, anxiety, and attention problems to our indoor lifestyle.[9] Obesity is a related time bomb. This detachment from natural surroundings could lead to dire consequences for the child's and the planet's health.

Another real threat in our noisy, overstimulating environment is anhedonia, or the inability to experience pleasure from once-enjoyable activities. This numbed response to life is becoming epidemic in our young. Dr. Dana McMakin suggested "the importance of working with youth to identify previously enjoyed activities and getting them moving toward old or new goals as a way to get them to change distorted negative thought patterns."[10] The best way to protect our children's minds from this lethargy is to guard their quiet and get them intentionally moving. How noisy is my child's world? I can talk one-on-one about what interests my child and encourage those passions. Becoming numb from noise is perhaps one of our children's greatest dangers that a calm environment and focused momentum can cure.

A common parenting philosophy for adolescents is to keep them busy and tired—never allow slack in the line. But the great danger is not just being motionless but being passive about their lives. Life is too fascinating to be dull, especially in young adulthood. Mark and I were not empathetic when our kids used the phrase "I'm bored." When they did, it was met with an activity that was more akin to hard work: here's the push broom for sweeping the driveway, you can help me with dinner, and grab the trash can and pull weeds. This counterattack almost always produced a burst of inspiration to find something better to do. It's hard to steer a parked car.

As parents, we can't be passive about our children's passivity. Children travel through awkward seasons, and new insecurities can paralyze our sensitive children into indecision and withdrawal. We want to be attentive to their real and imagined fears as well as our own. We can offer encouragement in tackling some new challenge and giving them real choices. No child is the consummate athlete or scholar or performing artist. But all kids need to feel competent in a few areas that they genuinely enjoy. And if the love tank is low, we can do favorite activities together.

Passivity also makes us, including our children, more gullible, to become victims instead of taking responsibility for our future. We float in the drift of culture, with hands off the tiller, when we need to be motoring for specific ports. We naively believe our circumstances will safely steer our course.

In the 1930s, one leader, Adolf Hitler, convinced his followers that Jewish people were dangerous. Listening to clever propaganda, Germany's citizens simply floated downstream as eleven million humans, including six million Jews, were exterminated.[11] Engaging in culture with our children may look threatening, but the consequences of withdrawal are much more ominous.

Let's be encouraged by our audacious goal. We are not fortifying our kids under siege of an invading, hostile culture. We are laying an inner foundation that will empower them to courageously enter and change their world. These tools will allow them to connect crossculturally with a wide spectrum of people and give them traction for forming new friendships. And relationships are what ultimately shape a culture.

We are all strapped into an exhilarating ride on a shrinking planet. Those young people who are outwardly focused with a global worldview will be able to enjoy and guide the journey for generations to come.

Questions

How would you describe your cultural literacy?

How can you practically give your child broader experiences in the arts or experience to history?

Do you have any exaggerated fears?

Are you ignoring any real threats to your child's purpose?

How can you help your child discover other cultures around the world?

Chapter 14

A HALLOWEEN PHOTO

Everyone Can Come to the Party

BY MARK

A safe fairyland is untrue to all worlds.

—J. R. R. Tolkien

We should have realized Halloween afternoon was a questionable time to have our newborn's photo taken. The hospital nursery camera failed to work the day of Jon's birth, so we got a coupon to have his "birth" picture taken a week later at a local photographer's studio. Apparently the world wasn't ready for him—yet.

As we pulled up to the address in a sketchy part of San Bernardino, we were shocked to find a long line of witches, werewolves, and goblins there to greet us. The studio was next door to a costume shop. Was it the world's trick or God's treat?

With our son swaddled protectively in our arms, as if guarding him from King Herod, we carried our nine-day-old Jon into a dark side street of San Bernardino. It seemed almost prophetic to carry our baby through this queue of hellish faces, not knowing the call on our sons' lives to enter some of the darker venues of culture. But it is the calling for all children: to invade this sometimes-scary world with the love, truth, goodness, and beauty of the God who made us.

Our natural instinct as parents is to protect our children. We want to shelter them physically, emotionally, and spiritually from all the goblins lurking in the dark. And so we do. But swaddling our kids indefinitely is not the safest and most productive way to live. Besides, it skips the best part: bringing friends to God's party.

Leaning into Culture

I was once encouraged to go down a double black diamond course, having just learned to ski the bunny slope. I was petrified. My friend's instructions? "Whatever you do, stay on your toes leaning forward; never lean back on your heels." So like Goofy sliding down the mountain with flailing arms and legs, I made the run safely, though it wasn't pretty. I'll never ski a double black diamond again, but it was good advice: stay on your toes, leaning forward.

The best defense is always a good offense, and we have the greatest offense imaginable: God's love for this world. So we are called to transform culture, not run from it. This offense keeps us in the most strategic, exhilarating place possible.

/// IF WE'VE RAISED OUR CHILDREN TO LIVE CREATIVELY ON THE EDGE, LOVING GOD'S WORLD, THEY WILL LIKELY BE DRAWN TO A PART OF THE WORLD THAT NEEDS THEIR LIGHT. /// At the same time, it may be an arena that frightens you as a parent. It's time to lean in.

Just Say No: Hierarchies and Walls

Two ideas can cripple our children from effectively loving their world. The first is a belief in an imaginary hierarchy that gives priority status to clergy, doctors, or other esteemed professionals deemed significant by our society. The other is a flawed ideal that builds a wall between the church and the world, the sacred and the secular.

We can falsely believe that priesthood or pastoring is the highest vocation for anyone serious about following God. We can emphasize this to children, saying, "*He's* the pastor, honey, who serves God full-time." But we rarely tell our children, "She serves God in her business," or, "He is a bright and loving light in our neighborhood." Our children will gravitate toward whatever we hold up as the ultimate standard. We are surrounded by pedestals, but if they are too high or ethereal, our kids will dismiss their own potential to serve.

Beyond teaching our children respect, we are indoctrinating them to believe that some folks are more important than others. Or in the words of George Orwell's *Animal Farm*, "Some animals are more equal than others." Our children are learning a spiritual hierarchy.

Since I was not raised in the church, I learned a different secular hierarchy. Medical doctors were kings because they possessed more knowledge and made more money. I wanted to be a doctor because they were wealthy, influential people.

This hierarchy mind-set is inescapable. There will always be the chiefs, medicine men, and warriors in any village. But if our children want to truly serve God (and they will), then we must stop imprinting them with this false idea that God uses only the elite—clergy, doctors, or even celebrities. We must erase and replace this notion with the new covenant's high watermark: we all have the Spirit (Joel 2:28), and we all are priests and kings who can uniquely serve God (1 Pet. 2:9).

We want our children to be bright lights in all aspects of culture: business, government, the arts, sports, and education. Kingdom heroes come in all sizes and shapes. Some have huge spheres of influence, while others much smaller. The measure of significance is not the size of the audience. God makes each one important in his or her assigned place. With that esteem, we all can move confidently into culture.

This frees our children to explore and try on different hats, knowing that all positions can play and are vitally important to God. This allows them to follow their hearts but also to treat others with dignity and respect. The ground is level in God's house.

Religious walls can also be an enormous hindrance to our children's purpose. In this narrative, the church is a protective castle separated by a moat from the world. Occasionally we must go *out there* to conduct business or reach *those people* not living in our fortress. But then we must quickly retreat behind the safe walls of fellowship.

This creates an unfortunate perspective of us versus them. A child raised with this thinking can adopt a missionary-compound mentality that fosters isolation. Sadly, the church ghetto is a large neighborhood. We must shovel the salt, including our kids, out of the church to be part of the community.

A child raised in a castle might find it hard to merge authentically with the masses later in life. Our children need to learn the art of "being in the world but not of it." It's best to start young by having relationships and friends with various beliefs, backgrounds, and interests. It helps our kids learn new complex social languages and prepares them for who they are becoming—vital contributors to culture and translators of God's message of love.

Presently in our home, and while our kids were small, we had this diversity of relationships, with folks who were believers and those who were not. They were all friends whom we genuinely loved and enjoyed. We couldn't imagine a party without them.

Labels Are Just Labels

Declaring something "Christian" does not automatically make it good for your child. Parents sometimes believe their children will be safer under that label. This is how the wall builders enforce their separatist ideal, by categorizing groups and events, like the nutritional disclosures on cereal boxes. We simply read the ingredients before we partake. But good can come out of Hollywood, New York, and Washington, DC, even as evil can exist in churches. Just because an approved sticker is attached doesn't mean it's spiritually healthy for our kids.

When Jon was nineteen, he and I were driving home from a concert where a Christian music label was looking for new talent. Jon expressed that he felt uncomfortable with the style of music, the parochial feel, and the aloofness of a few artists. As we sped seventy-five miles an hour down Interstate 5 to San Diego, he said, "I don't know what I think about Christian music. I don't know if we're a Christian band."

Just then, a car passed with an ICHTHUS fish on the back window. I pointed to the sticker and asked, "Is that a Christian car?" He laughed. I pressed further by saying that I didn't think a label made anything Christian. Only people can be Christians. The word is best used as a noun, not an adjective.

Yet we use the adjective a lot: Christian music, clubs, films, sports, and schools. It obviously can be helpful to identify believers under this heading. But the term is intended to refer to doctrine and purpose, not to culture. Unholy things happen in sacred places, and holy things can happen in secular places. All cultures, even within the church, are under God's scrutiny.

Similarly, Tim was asked years later in an interview if they were a Christian band. His response, wiser than my years, was, "We are Christians by faith, not genre." Labels can separate us from other people and deter folks from coming to the party. Entering culture is much more than slapping on a label. It's being genuinely interested in people and forming lifelong, redemptive friendships.

Restating the Purpose

Encouraging our children to enter and engage in culture is a fish or cut-bait moment. After a training course of almost twenty years, they are ready to test-drive their purpose in civilization. This is a moment of destiny for our children and the world.

Regardless of what occupation they choose, their vocation will be higher. Regardless of where they settle, their mission will go beyond the white picket fence American dream. Spontaneous or planned, individually and in groups, their calling is to live out the nature of

God in a particular setting. As Michael Green observed, what won over the hearts of the Roman Empire was how Christians lived. It was who they were, not just their message.[1]

This purpose goes beyond self-fulfillment, happiness, success, or even living boring, safe lives. Especially in adolescence, we want our kids to realize they play an essential part and they are greatly loved by God. In small and sometimes big ways, they are privileged to reflect God's face to those around them. They are not just writing their individual stories; they are part of the Great Story. We need to remind them of this often. Nothing could be more outlandishly significant.

Guides of the Cultural Jungle

Culture is like a jungle—it's easy to get lost. We need to find guides who know the jungle better than we do. I was fortunate to find a few, and so were my sons as they emerged into adulthood.

One of my literary guides was Richard Niebuhr. Through his seminal work, *Christ and Culture*, I understood that a believer could shift from an *against culture* position to an *into culture* approach.[2] If we are against culture, we just become separatists, but if we pour into culture, it can be transformational. We raised our kids with the hope of transforming their world because this was Jesus's approach, telling us to be salt and light in the world.

If we raise kids to only be against culture, we might create monsters: negative, suspicious, closed adults who perceive everything as a threat to their faith. But if our children are raised to make a contribution to this world, it births responsibility in them and a hope for redemption.

The risk is always present, that a child might get lost in the jungle, overtaken by greed and self-indulgence. But there is an equally great risk of forgetting their mission if they settle for the protective goals of safety and happiness. Raising children is not a risk-free enterprise. But if parents lovingly walk the jungle with their children from an early age, learning the paths, the risk is minimized and the reward is great.

Our sons were fortunate to have many guides, but one who stands out is Charlie Peacock. He was an early important influence, and still is. Charlie was their first producer and record president of Rethink. He not only believed in them musically but he also mentored them to thinking Christianly about all of life. He encouraged them to push the boundaries lyrically as well as through playing in venues where God belonged, outside church walls. Charlie wrote, "What does culture making maturity look like? It always concerns itself with quality over quantity.... I'm not only referring to musical quality, but to that unique quality associated with distinct Christian ways of being, doing, thinking, imagining, and loving."[3]

This is God's world, and His love belongs everywhere. That is the message of a faithful cultural guide. These mentoring relationships are critical in this final phase of childhood. Prayerfully consider who might guide your child through the jungle.

Pathways of the Culture Jungle

Our friends Tom and Janet left for Peru with their young children, wanting to make a difference in that country. Their goal was to make contact with a hidden people in the upper Amazon. Their hope was to bring them the love and truth of Jesus while preserving their culture and primitive lifestyle. The risks were high: disease, poisonous plants, snakes, caiman (crocodiles), and a possible hostile reaction from the aboriginal people.

It took years of patience and perseverance. They hoped to become friends by leaving gifts for the people. To leave those love gifts, they needed to learn what foods and tools were useful to the people, and find their jungle paths. It was on those pathways that relationships and trust were eventually established.

Although we live in an urban jungle, the principle is no different. Our modern jungle trails are education, business, sports, arts, media, government, social service, medicine, technology, and entertainment. If we want to make a redemptive impact, we must help our sons and daughters feel confident to travel these pathways with their cultural goods. We must be skilled at whatever we do, to leave a cultural good (a gift) that meets a need, and we must build loving relationships along the way. Without traveling these paths in the jungle, we risk irrelevancy and miss our purpose. We, as parents, must lead the way.

To paraphrase the gospel, we are simply raising our children to follow Jesus:

> For God loved sinners, prostitutes, tax collectors, and religiously proud people in such a way that He risked His own Son to show them His love. (John 3:16, my adaptation)

Jesus's messianic feasts with unholy guests incensed the religious leaders of His day. But it was our Lord who invited everyone to the party. He is our leader, so we want to follow. We want everyone at the table too.

Truth, Friendship, and a Good Cup of Coffee

The easiest way to help our children be an influence is to live that lifestyle ourselves. It really is that simple. We start with our neighborhoods, work associates, and places of play, making friends and learning how to best love each person. When children are raised in an outward-focused home, this interest in others becomes native to them.

Inevitably, our children will begin to express interests in various pathways of culture. We can quietly encourage these passions. Allow them to think Christianly about these interests without being sectarian. If they want to run for president, teach middle school, or be a pro surfer, let them describe what that could look like from a Christian worldview. How does knowing Christ influence how we participate in that setting?

/// THREE THINGS THAT WORK TOGETHER ARE ESSENTIAL FOR INFLUENCING CULTURE: TRUTH, FRIENDSHIP, AND GOODNESS. ///

Truth is our compass in the disorienting jungle. When the rainforest closes in and we lose the path, we can truth our way forward. We don't need to be opportunists who will do anything to be loved and popular. We want to be people of integrity and purpose, who won't sell our souls for votes or friends or business. We follow Truth Himself, and He keeps us free.

Truth is our asset, not our deficit. We can be trusted when our word is reliable and we are authentic. We never have to apologize for being truthful.

We also want to be good friends. I was speaking about this at a conference. In the Q and A, an honest person admitted that she did not know how to enter culture because she didn't know how to make a friend. We all want to improve our relationships. We rarely influence people we don't know.

Impacting this world means cultivating close friendships. It means caring without an agenda. People know when they are genuinely loved or not. Our Lord spent much of His time eating with friends who often had questionable pasts. To save the world, Jesus was a good friend. In fact, He was even a friend to Judas, right to the end.

The third influential ingredient is to actually create something good. This good does not mean fancy or flashy. It speaks of what is excellent, virtuous, and noble. We want to be known for our quality, in business, the arts, in friendship. Something that is cheap, flimsy, or shoddy will dampen any impact we might have had.

A believer has a different standard. Whatever we do, we do it for the glory of God (1 Cor. 10:31). If we make mediocre products, slapping on Jesus's name won't make them any better.

Charlie Peacock has said that if you're going to make coffee as a believer, then make a really good cup of coffee. Many coffeehouses popped up across the nation in the '70s, inviting confused youth to safe places to discuss life. The only negative was that they usually had horrible-tasting coffee. They cared only about spiritual things and neglected the obvious, tangible product. If Jesus Himself were running the place, the One who made all things good, He would offer a good cup of coffee. He was the One who saved the best wine for last.

In Search of Excellence was a business book of the '90s that stressed care and quality.[4] That's a great lesson for all who would enter culture. Care for the person and produce a quality product. We can model for our children to not just be an adequate carpenter, businessperson, artist, producer, minister, or attorney. Know your craft well. That will get people's attention.

Finding Their Niche

Chad Butler, the drummer of Switchfoot, was being interviewed by a radio DJ of a popular San Diego station just after the band's first album, *The Legend of Chin*, was released. The DJ said bluntly, "I can tell that the band's words are spiritual and pointing in a direction, but somehow I'm not offended, and find the lyrics accessible. As opposed to other Christian acts that I won't mention, such as …" and he went ahead to mention the name of a popular act with disdain. Chad responded wisely, not siding with the DJ's remark, by saying, "We're just trying to find our niche." That is what every child must do: find his or her own niche.

There are many variables to this equation—passion, talent, whom you know, opportunities, persistence, and grace. Having passion isn't enough without skill. Neither is being talented sufficient. Our kids need opportunities, people, and grace to open doors. We, as parents, can be another loving variable as we quietly cheer from the sidelines.

Plan B

This is a brutal reality: Not everyone can make a living doing what he or she loves. Occupation and vocation are different for a vast number of people. It is better to have that conversation early, so if our children are not able to survive on music, the fine arts, or some philanthropic passion, there is a backup plan.

Our world loves to cheer people on to their dreams. Young twentysomethings often want to restate that vision to their applauding audiences. It can turn into a campaign that becomes a success-or-failure scenario. If things don't go as planned, those brave risks can set up early stories of failure for young entrepreneurs. They have painted a public image of their dreams, but on the inside they have serious doubts and can feel defeated. Worse, they can even doubt God's faithfulness, believing their visions were do or die, not do and try.

What is success anyway? Families and individuals will define it differently. Does it mean having financial security, a second home, athletic achievement, or academic degrees? Or does it mean being with those you love and enjoying life together?

In some fields of culture, the success rate is quite small. Most musicians aren't entertainers or recording artists, but instructors. The same is unfortunately true of fine arts. Most aren't able to live off selling paintings and must make a living in commercial art or some other occupation. This is not failure. Rather, this is normal.

As a teenager, I wanted to be a career musician, but feedback from friends and family kept me in a dance band playing covers until a college sophomore. I also found God and switched my major from music to theology. Now when I hear my voice or piano playing, I'm glad for that dose of reality to change my course.

Having realistic conversations doesn't hurt the dream. It simply gives young adults parachutes as they fearlessly go into the stratosphere in their hot air balloons. We cheer and dream and hope, but we all know that backup plans exist. We can land these dreams safely.

I always encouraged my sons in their musical pursuits. I never imagined their efforts would turn into careers, but I did recognize that spark of creativity in their songwriting and performing. I was cautiously supportive, guiding them in buying used equipment but expecting them to keep up their studies and not bail on shifts at work. In fact, Tim was a coffee cart barista and Jon bused tables to pay for their first record. Playing music had a price tag.

/// **MOST OF LIFE IS NOT SUCCESS OR FAILURE, BUT BAD, GOOD, BETTER, AND BEST.** /// If I am not recognized as best by others, I have not failed. I am one human among many, not the Messiah. We simply find our niche and make a good cup of coffee. We leave the results to a sovereign God. We dream with an honest humility. Sometimes plan B stands for Best.

Unsung Heroes

On a recent trip to Italy, we spent a night in Assisi. We were awed by the positive difference one simple man, Saint Francis, made in his world. Francis rarely left his tiny hilltop village, but his historical footprint was huge.

The same could be said of William Wilberforce, George Washington Carver, Johann Sebastian Bach, Florence Nightingale, John Milton, Aleksandr Solzhenitsyn, and Mother Teresa. These were people who did not aim for greatness but simply offered a good cup of coffee and, in so doing, changed the world in some way.

Many people are trying to make a big cultural splash. They use social media, clever campaigns, and fierce marketing strategies to gain the most attention. Without doubting their motives, the question always has to be, what is the lasting fruit? I like to find heroes in hiding who didn't intend to make noticeable waves. These are the quiet, unsung (and sometimes sung) heroes who inspire me.

People are often impressed with our sons because of their fame or success. But that is not what impresses me. What I admire most are who they are, how they treat their friends, and how they use their coattails to influence the world with a story that is bigger than them.

I used to gently head butt my young sons, look them in the eyes, and say, "I want to grow up and be just like you." Now they have grown to be people who want to live for the good, the beautiful, and the true. More than ever, I still want to be like them.

Questions

How would you describe your own attitude toward current culture?

What is your family's engagement with culture right now?

Is there a friendship that needs nurturing outside the believing community?

Are there practical ways you can encourage your child to create some cultural good to share with others?

Chapter 15

SURFING THE HURRICANE

The Roaring Twenties

BY MARK

Our last day residing in Virginia Beach was spent packing and watching our sons surf Hurricane Bob. Although these weren't the largest or most dangerous waves they would eventually surf, it was certainly a moment of letting go. Tim and Jon, all of thirteen and fourteen, were surfing waves from a category-3 hurricane.

That was not our first surrender, nor would it be the last. Parenting involves progressive stages of releasing our children, allowing them freedom by inches to take calculated risks that lead to increased responsibility. As we watched nervously from shore, we knew that moving to California would be an even bigger risk than surfing Bob.

Off the Map

There is more literature in our modern culture about releasing one's inner child than about releasing our biological children. It seems that we are often underdeveloped adults still concentrating on our own fulfillment while ignorant, even negligent, about launching our biological children.

One evening, as I walked out of the ocean from a summer glass-off surf session, I saw four couples whom I recognized, enjoying dinner on blankets spread over the sand. After banter about waves and weather, they began to pepper me with questions.

One couple asked, "How did you raise your kids so that they wanted to live close and spend time with you as adults?" Another couple asked the opposite: "How did you get your kids to leave home? Ours are still here in their midtwenties!" One woman asked, "Why is it so hard for stay-at-home spouses who invest everything in their children, only to have the kids go off to college and forget you?"

Generational divides have shifted with the times. I'm guessing that adolescence only counted for one year in the '40s: sixteen. Then it lasted maybe seven years (thirteen to nineteen) in the '70s. Now, adolescence seems to begin at nine and end at twenty-nine. Our world hurries children to grow up but waits to release them. And no one is an expert on the process. Like Lewis and Clark, who realized their map of the Louisiana Territory was incomplete, many parents are missing information. We are off the map.

Family Life Cycle: Changing Roles

Launching is a wonderfully normal part of family life. Our children begin a new life cycle as young adults, become married, and then eventually have children, whom they raise and release. Then we move into the grandparent stage and our children eventually let go of us. Releasing our children allows us to see life from several perspectives. We watch our children leaving and our lives moving toward the latter part of life, as they see their own new cycle beginning.

With each new stage, there are often conflicts as we adjust to our new roles. Tension and misunderstandings are routine. But we must press through with love and open communication to discover our new normal.

Parents who release their children can feel demoted or unappreciated, especially if one spouse has stayed at home to raise the kids. The assignment we loved is suddenly over. We no longer cook for a crowd, attend school events, or set out lunch boxes. Our roles have changed dramatically.

In reality, good-bye begins the day a child is born, the moment the umbilical cord is cut. It continues when the child starts kindergarten, then intensifies in middle and high school. It reaches its crescendo when the child enters college or the workforce and eventually moves out. All the while, both parents are being stretched, adjusting to their changing responsibilities and relationships.

Similar to the parenting process, discipleship or mentoring can be simplified into four steps: (1) I do it; you watch; (2) I do it; you help me; (3) you do it; I help you; (4) you do it; I watch. If we have trained our children well, our roles in the relationship should change.

Early in our children's lives, we did everything for them as they watched. But if we were willing for more work initially, we let them help us—step two. Later, this help paid off; it increased their skills, built confidence, and strengthened our relationships. Late childhood and early adolescence is step three. We let our kids take more responsibilities while we encouraged. Launching is the transition from step three to step four. It demands our willingness to let go and watch. We've done our part; now it's their turn.

Someone once asked if I ever wanted to get up on the stage and play music when my sons are performing. My answer was absolutely not. This is my time to watch. This is a parent's ultimate reward, to see your children do things quite well without you.

Increased Freedom, Risk, and Responsibility

It seems like yesterday I was running behind to hold on to their two-wheel bikes, just liberated from training wheels. They rode with hair flying, without helmets. But they quickly caught on and were free to travel wherever those bikes could take them, though with new responsibilities.

/// INCREASED FREEDOM, INCREASED RISK, INCREASED RESPONSI-BILITY. THESE TRIUNE PRINCIPLES ACCOMPANY EVERY LAUNCH OF OUR CHILDREN. /// If only one or two are present, the process is incomplete. If only freedom is allowed without responsibility, the danger is quite high. There are serious consequences to society when parents release their children without having trained them in responsibility. If we haven't taught them freedom and responsibility on a playground, it's often too late to teach this in marriage or in a business office.

But if only responsibility is given without freedom, personal ownership is lost. Rebellion may occur because the rules are not their own. They may be adults in age, but they are still children at heart. Maturity requires responsibility under freedom of choice.

Risks are always present along the way. Gravity is as unforgiving as the economy or a diet. But if risk is mitigated in small stages of increased personal freedom and responsibility, it is minimized as much as possible by what the child learns through experience.

When our sons were in their midteens, they went backpacking with a youth leader who was an experienced outdoorsman. They were hiking through Tuolumne Meadows on the upper side of Yosemite over to Vernal Falls, then down to the Yosemite Valley. It was a strenuous four-day hike, with black bears raiding one kid's food because he hadn't seen the need to hang his backpack up high. We later saw pictures of their feet dangling 4,731 feet over the edge of Half Dome. Toward the end of the trip, Tim accidentally sliced his knee sliding down the stream above Vernal Falls and needed a medical helicopter to transport him back down to the valley.

When we got the call, we were concerned (panicked) and needed to know what was happening four hundred miles away, eight hours by car. But actually, the trip was perfect. No one was permanently injured, and our kids learned many life lessons. This trip combined the necessary freedom, risk, and responsibility for a middle teenager. But just like that startling call, early adolescence is usually a wake-up for parents to prepare for their children's fast-approaching independence.

Stairway to Heaven

When our sons were in junior high, they became interested in Led Zeppelin's music. I had played in bands throughout high school and into my freshman year of college, and we covered all the songs of that psychedelic era. Because some of my memories were not positive, I really struggled when my kids asked me to listen and play along. I wanted them to grow in their musical exposure but did not want that philosophy of irresponsible freedom with sex and drugs to be an influence. What should I do?

Instead of pulling back according to my fears and saying no, I leaned into the unwelcomed opportunity. I decided to encourage their innocent musical enthusiasm, while adding the understanding that we would discuss the lyrics so they could eventually learn discernment. As we talked about the meaning of the lyrics, they could decide what they would allow their ears to hear. I treated them with respect, rather than trying to control them. Increased freedom, increased risk, increased responsibility. Then I taught them "Stairway to Heaven."

It proved successful. They not only felt confident in their newly acquired musical prowess, but they also applied their love for cultural goodness to the lyrics as they chose what they would and wouldn't sing. One day, I popped into Jon's room where they were practicing and noticed a set list lying on the floor with a song crossed out. I inquired about that one song, and they answered, "Dad, you don't want to hear it. The words aren't great." Freedom, risk, and responsibility were giving them good ears. They were steering their own lives toward the true, good, and beautiful in the thick of rock culture.

Skipping College to Join a Band

I think growing up is harder on parents than their children. For kids, it's a wide-open world full of fascinating adventures. They don't yet know their limitations or mortality. The adults, on the other hand, know their children must make key decisions, as well as mistakes, and that some missteps can be irreversible. We want to transfer responsibility, but we don't want to instill fear.

Our sons enjoyed learning and did well academically. Taking advanced classes in high school allowed both of them to enter a good college as sophomores, on scholarship. This was what we had hoped for our sons, and their hard work had paid off.

Then came the band. They weren't seeking a label, just playing their original music in high school, then in college, under various names. Jon was a sophomore and Tim still a senior in high school when Charlie Peacock signed them to Rethink Records. At the time, the newly formed three-piece of Chad, Jon, and Tim was still playing in dorms, campus clubs, and small parties.

Charlie called to have a personal chat with me before he signed them. He told me he sensed Jon had a lot of songs in him but asked if I was ready for a record deal that could change the direction of their lives. I told him I thought I was. But it still was tough when their success required them to drop out of college.

Yes, it was hard for me. I pressed Tim to apply for another semester during the recording of *New Way to Be Human*. It was brutal for him to take classes during the week, then fly to Nashville on weekends to record. It was equally hard for Jon to be alone in Nashville tracking songs. Finally, I had to release my grip. I concluded that some people have their careers before college. I think Jon is still technically a senior and Tim a sophomore.

This was another letting go for me. It was not something any of us, including Jon and Tim, had planned, but sometimes life takes an unexpected turn and we need to let our kids follow the adventure.

Great Expectations

We celebrated with Chinese food the afternoon we learned Jan was pregnant with our first child. Her fortune cookie was prophetic: "Your horizons will be expanding to great proportions." Beyond the obvious physical dimension, our hearts were expanding to welcome this new life. We began to grow dreams about our child's future.

Watching a recent Olympics, I noticed two very different motivations for the men's all-around gymnasts. One kept saying he wanted to help his parents, and when he failed to win a medal, it wasn't personally disappointing but was framed as his failure to *them*. A doting father was constantly accompanying the other gymnast, whose close friendship with his dad was fuel for his final accomplishment, the bronze medal. One relationship felt toxic; the second seemed healthy and inspiring.

This raises the sticky issue of how we see our kids and how they see themselves. Our expectations can affect their dreams or their abilities to realize those ambitions in a healthy way. Even if we envision our son or daughter as a rising star, what will ultimately motivate him or her to reach for the sky? Is it truly our child's goal—or ours?

We must continually sift through the subtle (or obvious) nudges that we, as parents, can make along the way: Are you sure you want to choose that major … try out for that sport … cancel that interview … take the summer off? We want to have great expectations for our emerging adolescents, but allow only *their* visions to determine the specific shape.

The Art of Launching

Here are seven life lessons that Jan and I learned about releasing our children:

1. Love is liberating. From day one, we must learn to genuinely love through freedom. The goal is not to have our children regurgitate our answers but personally decide the best answer in a context of freedom. Just as God gave the first couple room to authenticate their love, we must do the same. We must learn to live on our toes and lean into freedom.

If the child is pushing against the boundaries, that is a signal. We want to be the ones pushing our children into strategic freedom, which is necessary to raise stallions. We are not raising plow horses.

The love modeled by God in the garden was authentic. /// LOVE AND CONTROL FIGHT AGAINST EACH OTHER, BUT LOVE AND TRUST HARMONIZE. /// Ultimate love must let go. Our children's love in return must not be coerced but freely given.

2. Overprotection smothers and stunts a child's development. Doting is not healthy. If we are enmeshed with our children, we need to put boundaries on ourselves.

We want to raise kids who can pull away from our apron strings. They need increasing distance to establish their own independent selves. Eventually, they will come to us, but allow them to initiate.

3. Learn to listen without giving advice. When our sons were little, we listened, then followed with an explanation: "That's because …" But as kids grow older, the less they want to hear our commanding voices. It's difficult not to share our vast wisdom, but if we overadvise, they will stop talking.

When they speak, we just listen, asking honest questions without manipulative angles. True friends don't have those contrived conversations. The more we sincerely listen, the more they will talk.

Both Jon and Tim have always talked openly with me. I know they don't share everything. Nobody does. But they still talk to me as the father-friend at coffee and out surfing. When they ask for advice, I give it. If they don't, I'm thrilled to just listen.

4. Love them by being interested in their passions. Many parents lose interest the moment their children pick paths that don't enthuse them. We are still missionaries to our adult-kids. We must continually learn about their world and love them with genuine attention.

I often will ask Jon and Tim about their musical world. There are so many gadgets in their studio I know nothing about and nuances of the music industry. Questions about their world show them I'm interested in who they are now. Sometimes it's what they want to talk about, and sometimes it's not. Silence allows them to take our conversations in directions that interest them.

5. Love their friends. As our kids grow older, they can sometimes bring home stray cats. These are people you might not choose as your best friend, but as our kids expand their horizons, they will naturally expand their relationships. Their lives are their own now, and we can learn to love their friends. If you are fortunate enough to have these unique persons within your walls, you have time-sensitive gifts. Listen to their stories; you may be surprised by what you learn.

6. Stop teaching with words. If your children don't know what you believe about God, family, and your nation by now, it's too late to convince them. Once they are adults—even earlier—we need to simply live our convictions. Sermonizing by parents is often despised as a controlling monologue, and it sucks all the oxygen from the air, causing our kids to bury their questions. Freedom of belief must be allowed even if it isn't an exact duplicate of ours.

7. Always welcome their phone calls and visits. Of course you're busy and doing something significant, but someone more important just walked into your life. These are your children, and you are their only parents. Whenever my kids come by for a visit, or need a conversation, it's time for me to hit pause.

Already but Not Yet

The twenties are like the kingdom of God—already here but not yet. They are old enough to make decisions that can permanently affect their world (and yours) for good or bad. Yet they are young and inexperienced enough to be unsure about themselves. They are not quite mature, and they know it. Some compensate for this in-between insecurity by being withdrawn. They are hesitant to step outside the house. Others compensate by acting overcompetent, as if they possess all knowledge. It can be extremely hard for parents to figure out their next move. We are needed one day and completely ignored the next.

Hopefully, if we have gradually increased their freedom, risk, and responsibility, it does not hit all at once, like stepping off a cliff. In the two-wheel-bike analogy, we move through steps toward bicycle independence. First came the tricycle, next with training wheels in front of the house, then in the neighborhood, and when ready, we run alongside, training wheels off. Finally, they are loose, creating their own balance and momentum. If we are still running alongside them with training wheels in the twenties, obviously their launch is not yet complete.

It takes courage to gradually open our hands and hearts to let go. Ann Landers wrote, "Some people believe holding on and hanging in there are signs of great strength. However, there are times when it takes much more strength to know when to let go and then do it."[1] We must intentionally look for opportunities at every age to take calculated risks. Like outgrowing shoes, our kids need bigger-sized responsibilities. We can't expect them to wake up one day with those adult shoes on their feet.

"They Behave as if We Don't Exist"

Some birds are not meant to be caged, that's all. Their feathers are too bright, their songs too sweet and wild. So you let them go, or when you open the cage to feed them they somehow fly out past you. And the part of you that knows it was wrong to imprison them in the first place rejoices, but still, the place where you live is that much more drab and empty for their departure.

—Stephen King, *Rita Hayworth and Shawshank Redemption*

A common grievance among parents whose children have moved on is they feel ignored or unappreciated. It can seem unfair that the more intentionally we've loved, the greater the loss will be felt. But encouragement lies in several positives. One is that launching is the goal. Having a forty-year-old child at home is not that special. We must not only release but also celebrate their independence.

Second, I can almost promise there will be better, kinder, more rewarding days ahead. A young adult will usually circle back around, drawing near in a different way. You have mothered and fathered your kids, and as they now face life's difficulties solo, they will become more grateful for the part you have played. /// **SOMEWHERE BETWEEN AGES TWENTY-FOUR AND THIRTY-TWO, THEY WILL WAKE UP IN APPRECIATIVE WONDER FOR YOUR INVESTMENT IN THEIR LIVES.** ///

And often they will bring back home new friendships, what they are learning in school, fresh inspiration for a career, potential spouses, or simply a book they want us to read. Our role is to listen quietly and give advice only when asked. They are testing these ideas or future relationships in the context of their family and home. These are free-association moments when we let them run with the line, without reeling them in. This will encourage many more conversations.

Quick advice or judgments will be equally judged with silence and distrust. Our openness signals to them that they can freely think out loud in our presence. Now we are not just parents but true friends. After the long parent-to-child journey, we have arrived at an adult-to-adult relationship. Of course, we are still their parents emotionally, but in practical terms, only by invitation. One friend described it this way: they can freely raid your refrigerator whenever they want, but you can only open theirs by permission.

Invisible Encouragers

Often what happens behind the scenes is the most critical. We have enjoyed our starring role with a visible, speaking part but now find ourselves watching silently from the wings. Our place now, as always, is to be invisible encouragers.

In this inconspicuous role, we have ongoing responsibilities. We can touch our children's lives through prayer. Many times in our conversations with God, or even through dreams, Jan and I have become aware of specific needs. Being a continent away is no obstacle for this supernatural influence. Daily, and throughout the day, we talk to God about our kids.

Simply being available is also a prized gift to our adult children. We continue the yes of childhood, never saying no to opportunities to be present when they need us. We continue the positive encouragement that was so shaping in their formative years. Our words can still have great impact.

Saying Good-bye

Good-bye was different for us.

We said good-bye when each one moved off to college. Both wanted to live on campus even though they were twenty miles from home. It was a great decision.

Good-byes came often when touring began. They would live at home for months, then be gone for months. They were grown men, traveling the world, negotiating with attorneys, managers, and producers, yet still my sons. It was an awkward stage that no one warned me about: almost gone but independent and sometimes living at home.

I struggled through that period, not knowing my role or theirs and what a family should look like at that stage. We were three stags living under one roof. But there were also rich, surprising blessings. It was our sons' roaring twenties. In retrospect, I wished I would have relaxed more and enjoyed the ride.

When a wave holds you down in surfing, here is good advice: Just relax and let the wave drag you along the bottom. Don't waste air and energy fighting something bigger than you. I wish I had done exactly that under the big waves of letting go. This final release was the hardest. The twenties seemed more difficult than the teens.

I relished every time they invited me into their crazy lives: popping into the studio, traveling and surfing when we could. Music, surfing, and spirituality were our bonds still. As an outspoken leader, I found a softer voice and gained a better relationship by using my ears. Sadly and wonderfully, they were both fully launched in their early twenties.

A New Good

This life stage brings a new but different good. Parents who've had an incredible child-raising journey can tend to focus on the rearview mirror, staring at those meaningful good old days. But these same memories, though cherished, provide the foundation for a new good. Throughout the adventure of letting go is the anticipation that an extraordinary adventure awaits us. The same God who gave the previous good will also give us the new.

Launching Eagles

A bald eagle can take its first flight at about ten to fourteen weeks after hatching, when its down is replaced with juvenile feathers. The parents stir the young eagle to fly by leaving the nest mostly empty, then returning with empty talons. The pain of hunger and loneliness becomes a motivator. The eaglet must take responsibility for its own survival. It must become a bird that not only nests and eats but flies.

The young eagle often resists this ownership and even loses weight, while the parents fly past, providing an example by flapping their wings. Sometimes in flight, the parent will dangle a small rodent to lure the eaglet to spread its wings and come to the edge of the nest. For several weeks, the eaglets progress to spending increased time on branches near the nest, often flapping their wings. Finally, a strong updraft fills the bird's wings, it catches lift, and for the first time, the eagle begins to soar.

For the next four to five weeks, the adolescent will take short flights, occasionally pouncing on a rodent or fish to practice its hunting skills. During the day the adolescents are perched farther and farther from the nest. Finally comes the day the young adult eagle is fully launched, never to return to that nest.

The first flight of a bald eagle affects its life forever. Just as humans must pass certain cultural rites of passage in growing from childhood to adolescence to adulthood, the bald eagle must take its first flight away from the nest and learn to fend for itself in the wild before it finally takes on the plumage and the responsibilities of the adult eagle at about four or five years of age. The site of this first flight or fledging will be where the bald eagle later returns to nest and raise its own young.

There is wonderful joy in watching our sons soar higher than we ever have. And now we see them hatch new eaglets in their own nests with the intent of launching and soaring.

This is every parent's dream. We hope to launch eagles.

Questions

What are some specific ways you can encourage your child's independence?

What is one area in your child's life that you can release? What could that look like? Do you need to have a conversation with your child to build an adult-to-adult, rather than a parent-to-child, relationship?

What do you appreciate most about your child? Tell your son or daughter this week.

NOTES

Chapter 1: Hey, Can That Kid Swim?

1. Rick Weissbourd et al., *The Children We Mean to Raise: The Real Messages Adults Are Sending about Values*, Making Caring Common Project, Harvard Graduate School of Education, July 2, 2014, accessed January 26, 2015, http://sites.gse.harvard.edu/sites/default/files/making-caring-common/files/mcc_report_7.2.14.pdf.

2. Roy F. Baumeister et al., "Does High Self-Esteem Cause Better Performance, Interpersonal Success, Happiness, or Healthier Lifestyles?," *Journal of Psychological Science in Public Interest* 4, no. 1 (May 2003): 1, accessed January 26, 2015, www.psychologicalscience.org/journals/pspi/pdf/pspi411.pdf; and Eddie Brummelman, "'That's Not Just Beautiful—That's Incredibly Beautiful!' The Adverse Impact of Inflated Praise on Children with Low Self-Esteem," *Psychological Science*, March 12, 2014, accessed January 26, 2015, http://pss.sagepub.com/content/early/2014/01/15/0956797613514251.abstract.

3. Henry Cloud and John Townsend, *Raising Great Kids: A Comprehensive Guide to Parenting with Grace and Truth* (Grand Rapids, MI: Zondervan, 1999).

4. Philip B. Dembo, *The Real Purpose of Parenting: The Book You Wish Your Parents Read* (Los Angeles: Jacquie Jordan, 2011).

5. Brenda L. Volling, Annette Mahoney, and Amy J. Rauer, "Sanctification of Parenting, Moral Socialization, and Young Children's Conscience Development," *Psychology of Religion and Spirituality* 1 (February 2009): 53–68, accessed January 26, 2015, www.ncbi.nlm.nih.gov/pmc/articles/PMC3124783/; "Helping Children Build a Conscience," *The Successful Parent* (blog), July 19, 2001, accessed January

26, 2014, www.thesuccessfulparent.com/moral-development/helping-children -build-a-conscience; Grazyna Kochanska and Nazan Aksan, "Children's Conscience and Self-Regulation," *Journal of Personality* 74, no. 6 (December 2006), accessed January 26, 2015, www.psy.miami.edu/faculty/dmessinger/c_c/rsrcs/rdgs/emot /kochanskaaksan2006.conscienceoverview.pdf; and Marvin W. Berkowitz and John H. Grych, "Fostering Goodness: Teaching Parents to Facilitate Children's Moral Development," *Journal of Moral Education* 27, no. 3 (1998): 371–91, accessed January 26, 2015, http://parenthood.library.wisc.edu/Berkowitz/Berkowitz.html.

6. William Shakespeare, *Henry the Eighth*, prologue and act 3, scene 1 ("goodness' sake"). Then adapted to "Good for goodness' sake" in John Frederick Coots and Haven Gillespie's "Santa Claus Is Coming to Town" (1934).

Chapter 2: Our Long, Winding Road

1. Kathleen M. Galvin, Carma L. Bylund, and Brandon Grill, "Genograms: Constructing and Interpreting Interaction Patterns," Genograms.org, accessed January 26, 2015, www.genograms.org/index.html.

2. Mergan Naidoo, "Family Systems: Genograms and Ecomaps," Anti Essays, accessed January 26, 2015, www.antiessays.com/free-essays/Ecosystemic -Psychology-503216.html.

3. "Vasa (ship)," *Wikipedia*, last modified January 19, 2015, http://en.wikipedia.org /wiki/Vasa_(ship).

Chapter 3: I Enjoy You

1. J. B. Phillips, *Your God Is Too Small: A Guide for Believers and Skeptics Alike* (New York: Touchstone, 2004), 31.

2. D. Ross Campbell, "The Foundation," chap. 3 in *How to Really Love Your Child* (Wheaton, IL: Victor Books, 1977).

3. Rudolf Dreikurs and Vicki Soltz, "The Child's Mistaken Goals," chap. 4 in *Children: The Challenge* (New York: Plume, 1990).

Chapter 4: Matching T-Shirts

1. Stephen R. Covey, *The 7 Habits of Highly Effective People: Powerful Lessons in Personal Change* (New York: Free Press, 2004), 298.

2. Charles E. Hummel, *Tyranny of the Urgent*, rev. ed. (Downers Grove, IL: InterVarsity, 1994), 4.

3. Henry Cloud and John Townsend, *Raising Great Kids: A Comprehensive Guide to Parenting with Grace and Truth* (Grand Rapids, MI: Zondervan, 1999), 26.

Chapter 5: Knock Off, Baby

1. James E. Loder, *The Logic of the Spirit: Human Development in Theological Perspective* (San Francisco: Jossey-Bass, 1998), 91.

2. Henry Cloud and John Townsend, *Raising Great Kids: A Comprehensive Guide to Parenting with Grace and Truth* (Grand Rapids, MI: Zondervan, 1999), 68.

3. James E. Loder, *The Transforming Moment*, 2nd ed. (Colorado Springs: Helmers & Howard, 1989), 175.

4. Cloud and Townsend, *Raising Great Kids*, 29.

5. Rick Nauert, "Modeling Behavior for Children Has Long-Lasting Effects," Psych Central, May 28, 2010, accessed January 26, 2015, http://psychcentral.com/news /2010/05/27/modeling-behavior-for-children-has-long-lasting-effects/14139.html.

6. Rick B. van Baaren et al., "Mimicry for Money: Behavioral Consequences of Imitation," *Journal of Experimental Social Psychology* 39 (2003): 393–98, accessed January 26, 2015, www.uni-muenster.de/imperia/md/content/psyifp/aeechterhoff /wintersemester2011-12/vorlesungkommperskonflikt/van_baaren_etal_mimicry_ for_money_jesp2003.pdf.

Chapter 6: Creative Space

1. C. S. Lewis, *Surprised by Joy: The Shape of My Early Life* (Orlando: Harvest, 1955), 207.

2. "Media and Children," American Academy of Pediatrics, accessed January 27, 2015, www.aap.org/en-us/advocacy-and-policy/aap-health-initiatives/Pages

/Media-and-Children.aspx; and "TV and Children: Television, Health and Development," University of Washington, accessed January 27, 2015, http://depts.washington.edu/tvhealth/materials/third-party-resources/TV-Children -Television-Health-Development.pdf.

3. Jane M. Healy, "Endangered Minds," in *Creating the Future: Perspectives on Educational Change*, comp. and ed. Dee Dickinson (Baltimore, MD: New Horizons for Learning, 2002), at Johns Hopkins School of Education, accessed January 27, 2015, http://education.jhu.edu/PD/newhorizons/future/creating_the_future/crfut _healy.cfm.

4. Christo Pantev et al., "Increased Auditory Cortical Representation in Musicians," *Nature*, April 23, 1998.

5. Daniel J. Levitin, *This Is Your Brain on Music: The Science of a Human Obsession* (New York: Dutton, 2006), 191.

6. "Piano and Computer Training Boost Student Math Achievement, UC Irvine Study Shows," Today at UCI, March 15, 1999, accessed January 27, 2015, http://archive .today.uci.edu/news/release_detail.asp?key=646.

7. "Profile of SAT and Achievement Test Takers," College Board, comp. Music Educators National Conference, 2001, cited in "How Music Can Dramatically Affect Your Child's Development and Life-Time Success," Foundation for Music Literacy, accessed January 27, 2015, www.sonlight.com/uploads/children-and -music-research.pdf.

8. Howard Gardner, "Musical Intelligence," chap. 6 in *Frames of Mind: The Theory of Multiple Intelligences* (New York: Basic Books, 2011).

9. Associated Press, "Coast Guard Rescues Two Injured Sailors in San Francisco" *USA Today*, April 2, 2012, accessed January 27, 2015, http://usatoday30.usatoday .com/news/military/story/2012-04-01/yacht-race-rescue/53936036/1.

Chapter 7: Pizza with God

1. Ralph Waldo Emerson, *Letters and Social Aims*, rev. ed., Emerson's Complete Works, vol. 8 (Boston: Houghton, 1886), 95.

2. C. S. Lewis, "Sometimes Fairy Stories May Say Best What's to Be Said," in *Of Other Worlds: Essays and Stories* (San Diego: Harvest, 1994), 37.

Chapter 8: Thank You for Passing the Salt

1. Anne Ortlund, *Children Are Wet Cement* (Grand Rapids, MI: Revell, 1981).

Chapter 9: A Broken Wooden Spoon

1. Committee for Children (2004), quoted in "Child Discipline," American Humane Association, accessed January 28, 2015, www.americanhumane.org/children/stop-child-abuse/fact-sheets/child-discipline.html.

2. *The Brown-Driver-Briggs Hebrew and English Lexicon* (Peabody, MA: Hendrickson, 1996), s.v. "discipline."

3. Derek Kidner, *Proverbs: An Introduction and Commentary*, Tyndale Old Testament Commentary Series (Downers Grove, IL: InterVarsity, 1984), 147.

4. Sheryl Eberly and Caroline Eberly, *365 Manners Kids Should Know: Games, Activities, and Other Fun Ways to Help Children and Teens Learn Etiquette*, rev. ed. (New York: Three Rivers, 2011), 1.

5. Elizabeth T. Gershoff, *Report on Physical Punishment in the United States: What Research Tells Us about Its Effects on Children* (Columbus, OH: Center for Effective Discipline, 2008), accessed January 28, 2015, http://resources.med.fsu.edu/vdca/data/papers/pro-res/es001.pdf, 7.

6. For more on this, read Chip Ingram, *Effective Parenting in a Defective World: How to Raise Kids Who Stand Out from the Crowd* (Carol Stream, IL: Tyndale, 2006).

7. C. S. Lewis, *The Weight of Glory: And Other Addresses* (New York: HarperCollins, 2001), 26.

8. Kevin Leman, *Making Children Mind without Losing Yours* (Grand Rapids, MI: Revell, 2000), 15.

Chapter 10: The Company We Keep

1. "Profile America: Facts for Features," United States Census Bureau, March 19, 2012, accessed January 28, 2015, www.census.gov/newsroom/releases/archives/facts_for_features_special_editions/cb12-ff08.html.

2. "Children in Single-Parent Families," Kids Count Data Center, accessed January 29, 2015, http://datacenter.kidscount.org/data/tables/106-children-in-single-parent-families#detailed/1/any/false/868,867,133,38,35/any/429,430.

3. Edith Schaeffer, *What Is a Family?* (Grand Rapids, MI: Raven's Ridge Books, 1975), 201.

4. Diane Severance, "Susanna Wesley: Christian Mother," Christianity.com, accessed January 29, 2015, www.christianity.com/church/church-history/timeline/1701-1800/susanna-wesley-christian-mother-11630240.html; and *The Westminster Collection of Christian Quotations: Over 6,000 Quotations Arranged by Theme*, comp. Martin H. Manser (Louisville: Westminster John Knox, 2001), 253.

5. Robert Elliott Gonzales, *Poems and Paragraphs* (Columbia, SC: The State Company, 1918), 182.

6. Michael Akers and Grover Porter, "What Is Emotional Intelligence (EQ)?," Psych Central, accessed January 29, 2015, http://psychcentral.com/lib/what-is-emotional-intelligence-eq/0001037.

Chapter 11: Mystery Waffles and Paddleboards

1. Les Krantz and Chris Smith, "Our Eating Habits," in *The Unofficial U.S. Census: Things the Official U.S. Census Doesn't Tell You about America* (New York: Skyhorse, 2011).

2. "Tom Blake: Riding the Breakers on This Hollow Hawaiian Surfboard," *Popular Mechanics*, July 1937, 114–17.

Chapter 12: Raising Analog Kids in a Digital World

1. See for example Kaveri Subrahmanyam and David Smahel's *Digital Youth: The Role of Media in Development* (New York: Springer, 2012).

2. Marc Prensky, "Digital Natives, Digital Immigrants," *On the Horizon* 9, no. 5 (October 2001).

3. Larry D. Rosen, "Poke Me: How Social Networks Can Both Help and Harm Our Kids," *Monitor* 42, no. 9 (October 2011).

4. Stuart Brown, "What Is Play, and Why Do We Do It?," chap. 2 in *Play: How It Shapes the Brain, Opens the Imagination, and Invigorates the Soul* (New York: Avery, 2009).

5. Jeannine Ouellette, "The Death and Life of American Imagination," *Rake*, October 16, 2007, accessed January 29, 2015, www.rakemag.com/2007/10/death -and-life-american-imagination; Rhonda Clements, "An Investigation of the Status of Outdoor Play," *Contemporary Issues in Early Childhood* 5, no. 1 (2004); Dorothy G. Singer and Jerome L. Singer, eds., *Handbook of Children and the Media* (Thousand Oaks, CA: Sage, 2001); and Kenneth R. Ginsburg, "The Importance of Play in Promoting Healthy Child Development and Maintaining Strong Parent-Child Bonds," *Pediatrics* 119, no. 1 (January 2007).

6. Subrahmanyam and Smahel, *Digital Youth*, 51.

7. Ed Miller, quoted in Ouellette, "Death and Life."

8. Ouellette, "Death and Life."

9. Dana Gioia, quoted in Ouellette, "Death and Life."

10. Kyung Hee Kim, "The Creativity Crisis: The Decrease in Creative Thinking Scores on the Torrance Tests of Creative Thinking," *Creativity Research Journal* 23, no. 4 (2011): 285–95.

11. "About Montessori," Kennebec Montessori School, accessed January 29, 2015, www.kennebecmontessori.org/html/about_montessori.html.

12. Molly Ames Baker, quoted in Kate Bassett, "New Technology or Imagination: Finding That Balance," *Harbor Light Newspaper*, at Getting Kids Outdoors, accessed January 29, 2015, www.gettingkidsoutdoors.org /new-technology-or-imagination-finding-that-balance.

13. "Children, Adolescents, and the Media," *Pediatrics*, October 28, 2013, accessed January 29, 2015, http://pediatrics.aappublications.org/content/early/2013/10/24 /peds.2013-2656.

14. Ginsburg, "Importance of Play," 182–91.

15. Ginsburg, "Importance of Play," 182–91.

16. Subrahmanyam and Smahel, *Digital Youth*, 136.

17. Rosen, "Poke Me."

18. Subrahmanyam and Smahel, *Digital Youth*, 136.

19. Subrahmanyam and Smahel, *Digital Youth*, 135.

20. Subrahmanyam and Smahel, *Digital Youth*, 131.

21. Subrahmanyam and Smahel, *Digital Youth*, 127–28.

22. C. S. Lewis, *The Weight of Glory: And Other Addresses* (New York: HarperCollins, 2001), 45–46.

23. Pope Francis, quoted in Steve Scherer, "Pope Urges Young People Not to Waste Time on Internet and Smartphones," Reuters, August 6, 2014, accessed January 29, 2015, http://in.reuters.com/article/2014/08/05/pope-youth-internet-idINKBN0G5 2K520140805.

24. Bassett, "New Technology."

25. Bassett, "New Technology."

26. Bassett, "New Technology."

27. Cris Rowan, "10 Reasons Why Handheld Devices Should Be Banned for Children under the Age of 12," *Huffington Post* (blog), October 1, 2014, accessed January 29, 2015, www.huffingtonpost.com/cris-rowan/10-reasons-why-handheld -devices-should-be-banned_b_4899218.html.

28. "Daily Media Use among Children and Teens Up Dramatically from Five Years Ago," Kaiser Family Foundation, January 20, 2010, accessed January 29, 2015, http://kff.org/disparities-policy/press-release/daily-media-use-among-children -and-teens-up-dramatically-from-five-years-ago/.

29. Stuart and Jill Briscoe (lecture, North Coast Calvary Chapel, fall 2013).

30. Subrahmanyam and Smahel, *Digital Youth*, 51.

31. Robin M. Kowalski et al., "Bullying in the Digital Age: A Critical Review and Meta-analysis of Cyberbullying Research among Youth," *Psychological Bulletin* 140, no. 4 (July 2014): 1073–1137, accessed January 29, 2015, http://psycnet.apa.org /index.cfm?fa=search.displayRecord&uid=2014-04307-001; and Corrie L. Jackson

and Robert Cohen, "Childhood Victimization: Modeling the Relation between Classroom Victimization, Cyber Victimization, and Psychosocial Functioning," *Psychology of Popular Media Culture* 1, no. 4 (October 2012): 254–69, accessed January 29, 2015, http://psycnet.apa.org/journals/ppm/1/4/254/.

32. Subrahmanyam and Smahel, *Digital Youth*, 132.

Chapter 13: The Discerning Consumer

1. C. S. Lewis, *De Descriptione Temporum: An Inaugural Lecture* (Cambridge: Cambridge University Press, 1955), 23. It was delivered on November 29, 1954.

2. C. S. Lewis, *Surprised by Joy: The Shape of My Early Life* (Orlando: Harcourt, Brace, Jovanovich, 1955), 207–8.

3. C. S. Lewis, "On the Reading of Old Books," in *God in the Dock* (Grand Rapids, MI: Eerdmans, 2014), 220.

4. Thomas Dubay, *The Evidential Power of Beauty: Science and Theology Meet* (San Francisco: Ignatius, 1999).

5. American Revolution Center, *The American Revolution. Who Cares?: Americans Are Yearning to Learn, Failing to Know* (Washington, DC: American Revolution Center, 2009), accessed January 29, 2015, http://amrevmuseum.org/sites/default/files/attachment/ARCv27_web.pdf; and Andrew Romano, "How Ignorant Are Americans?," *Newsweek*, March 20, 2011, accessed January 29, 2015, www.newsweek.com/how-ignorant-are-americans-66053.

6. Muriel Strode, "Wind-Wafted Wild Flowers," *Open Court*, January 1903, 505.

7. Haim G. Ginott, *Between Parent and Teenager* (New York: Avon Books, 1969), 18.

8. G. K. Chesterton, *What's Wrong with the World* (New York: Dodd, Mead, and Company, 1912), 320.

9. Richard Louv, *Last Child in the Woods: Saving Our Children from Nature-Deficit Disorder* (Chapel Hill, NC: Algonquin Books, 2008), 10.

10. Dana L. McMakin, quoted in "New TORDIA Data Suggests Anhedonia an Important Target for Early Treatment," *Child and Adolescent Psychopharmacology Update*, Brown University, April 24, 2012, accessed January 29, 2015, www.childadolescentpsychopharm.com/Article-Detail

/new-tordia-data-suggests-anhedonia-an-important-target-for-early-treatment
.aspx.

11. *Encyclopedia Britannica Online*, s.v. "Holocaust," last modified July 17, 2014, accessed January 29, 2015, www.britannica.com/EBchecked/topic/269548/Holocaust.

Chapter 14: A Halloween Photo

1. Michael Green, "Conversion," chap. 6 in *Evangelism in the Early Church*, rev. ed. (Grand Rapids, MI: Eerdmans, 2004).

2. H. Richard Niebuhr, *Christ and Culture* (New York: Harper, 1951).

3. Charlie Peacock, "Embracing a Larger View of Worship," ChurchLeaders.com, accessed January 30, 2015, www.churchleaders.com/worship/worship-articles/139854
-culture-and-christianity.html.

4. Thomas J. Peters and Robert H. Waterman Jr., *In Search of Excellence: Lessons from America's Best-Run Companies* (New York: Harper and Row, 1982).

Chapter 15: Surfing the Hurricane

1. "Ann Landers Quotes," Goodreads, accessed January 30, 2015, www.goodreads.com
/quotes/17642-some-people-believe-holding-on-and-hanging-in-there-are.